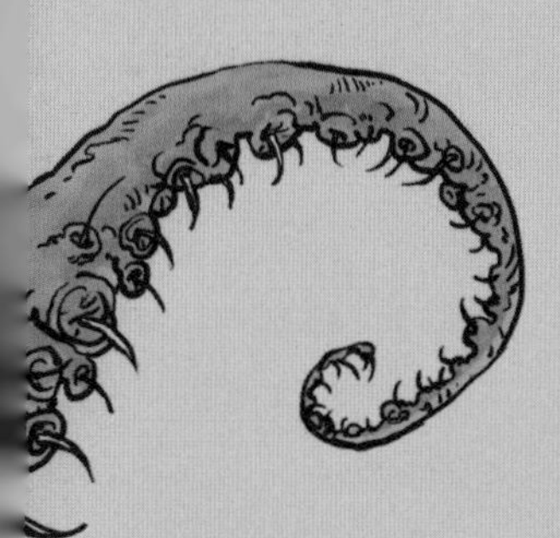

MONSTERS

100 WEIRD CREATURES FROM AROUND THE WORLD

For Cal and Mae, and for all the resilient and brave children out there.

Thanks also to Ray Harryhausen, Scooby-Doo and Boris Karloff for filling our young minds with fascination and frights.

SB and QW, November 2020

First published in Great Britain in 2021
by Wren & Rook

HB ISBN: 978 1 5263 6349 7
E-book ISBN: 978 1 5263 6350 3

10 9 8 7 6 5 4 3 2 1

Wren & Rook, an imprint of
Hachette Children's Group
Part of Hodder and Stoughton
Carmelite House
50 Victoria Embankment
London EC4Y 0DZ

An Hachette UK Company
www.hachette.co.uk
www.hachettechildrens.co.uk

Publishing Director: Debbie Foy
Senior Editor: Corinne Lucas
Art Director: Laura Hambleton
Senior Designer: Sophie Gordon
Designer: Pete Clayman

Printed and bound in China

Sarah Banville *Quinton Winter*

MONSTERS

100 Weird Creatures from Around the World

wren & rook

CONTENTS

INTRODUCTION

In the moment between the light switching off and on, in the area just behind you that you never see and in those unknown places that you dare not visit, that is where the monsters live.

Are you ready to step into one hundred mysterious, ridiculous and fantastical stories to meet the world's finest selection of bizarre creatures? You don't mind slime, mud, dribble, stench, poo and guts, do you? Because this journey is not for the squeamish. It will take you around the world, trekking across mountains in search of the wild men: Bigfoot, Yeti, Basajaun and Ucumar-Zupai. You'll dive into the oceans where the water giants lurk: Kraken, Crabzilla, Ningen and Lusca. Setting up camp in forests, you'll be surrounded by the screams and howls of Wendigo, the Jersey Devil, the Beast of Gévaudan and Yara Ma Yha Who! Do you dare to enter the deep cave lairs of Lou Carcolh, Trolls, Grootslang and Ho Tinh? And you will visit the hushed towns that are terrorised by Gulyabani, the Loveland Frog, Jiangshi and Mothman.

These beautiful, imaginative beasts rose from storytelling, which people created to try to understand mysteries. They teach us about lost lands and lost people. They are made from misunderstandings and superstitions, monstrously filling in the gaps in our knowledge before scientific discoveries stepped in.

We love monsters because we love to be scared. We love that these strange oddities teach us about history, science and geography. But more than that, they teach us about bravery – how people explore the world and face their fears; creativity – how writers and storytellers conjured up the unimaginable; and love – because many of these monsters were created to protect those we cherish from coming to harm. These wonderful creations show that we are very similar now to the people who lived hundreds, and sometimes thousands, of years ago, when lots of these monsters first appeared. They show that we value our home, family and survival above all else.

Following in monstrous footsteps, fuelled by your curiosity, you are about to bound across continents and come face-to-fang with unimaginable things, things you would never believe.

Love the unknown, because it encourages adventure, expedition, scientific knowledge, imagination and possibility.

**We promise to disgust, amuse and captivate you.
Come on in. Come and meet the monsters ...**

Alongside each monster's name you will see where they come from, other names they are known by and symbols, which tell you a little more about the monster's origins and history.

Folklore: The stories, beliefs and history of these monsters have been shared by spoken words, which pass on lessons and experiences for generations.

Myth: The fictional tales and legends of these supernatural creatures and gods are widely believed and have been passed on by written or spoken words.

Sightings: There have been real personal experiences of meeting these monsters, including seeing, smelling, hearing or feeling their presence.

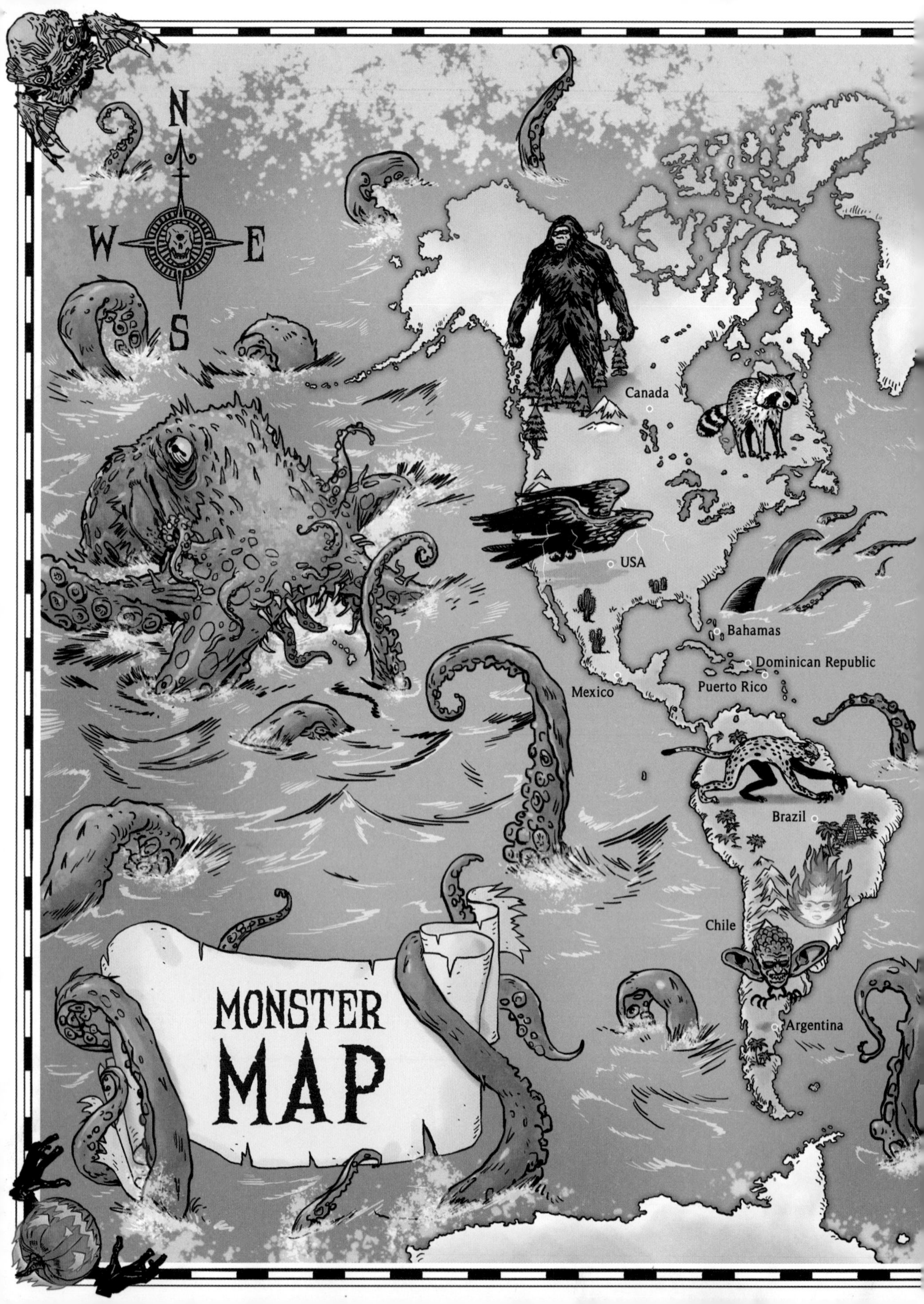
N
W
E
S
Canada
USA
Bahamas
Dominican Republic
Puerto Rico
Mexico
Brazil
Chile
Argentina
MONSTER
MAP

Arctic
Iceland
Norway
Sweden
Finland
Scotland
reland
Denmark
England
Belgium
Poland
Germany
Czech Republic
France
Spain
Italy
Portugal
Greece
Turkey
Iraq
Israel
Egypt
Russia
Mongolia
Persia
Pakistan
Arabia
India
Nepal
China
North Korea
Japan
South Korea
Thailand
Vietnam
Philippines
Singapore
Indonesia
The Gambia
Congo River Basin
Zambia
Madagascar
South Africa
Australia
Fiji
New Zealand
Antarctica

BIGFOOT

OTHER NAMES Dewey Lake Monster, Mogollon Monster, Sasquatch

USA

You find yourself travelling at night along the winding roads of the USA's Pacific Northwest. You're taking in the sights that this heavily wooded and beautifully wild area has to offer. Driving along the unlit roads, the car's headlights search into the darkness. Fog clings to the towering pine trees at the road's edge. Could there be someone out there?

STOP! What was that? You swear you saw something in the trees. Sightings of a beast have been recorded in this area for over 1,000 years. Eyewitness accounts, drawings and film footage all describe the same characteristics: an upright creature about 3 metres tall, with dark fur, teeth and claws, leaving five-toed footprints that are as long as your leg! Did you just glimpse Bigfoot?

You wouldn't be the first. Bigfoot has been hunted for decades. There have been many famous hoaxes; people in ape costumes pretending to be Bigfoot, faked physical evidence and even complete bodies encased in ice. But for as many hoaxes, there are good people, like you, who swear they have encountered this monster. Looking out, you see masses of wild forest to hide in. You could spend your life tracking Bigfoot, only to end up finding your own footsteps in the dirt.

The Native Americans call him Sasquatch, and he seems to have relatives. In 1964 there were many sightings of the Dewey Lake Monster, a 3-metre Bigfoot spotted swimming in Lake Dewey. Not forgetting the 2-metre smelly Mogollon Monster, who throws stones, makes nests in trees and whistles a warning. You do not want to hear that awful whistle as you stroll under the trees.

Is Bigfoot a large ape? A leftover early human from millions of years ago, roaming lonely and lost in this modern age? There has been no scientific proof of his existence, but of course we all know that science cannot prove everything.

The car headlights illuminate a huge creature at the bend in the road. He stares at you with burning red eyes. Seconds later he is gone. Was it him? Was it Bigfoot?

YARA MA YHA WHO

AUSTRALIA

It is so hot. Even in the shade of the fig trees, the temperatures soar and the heat's haze makes you sleepy. You check the map so you know where you are in the dense, sweet-smelling forest, near the Pacific Coast of Australia.

The leafy canopy above rustles. A few dried leaves fall, and you look up past the figs and into the higher branches. What is that? There! Red, deep red like burning fire, and crouching on the branch! Frog-like, big-headed, big-bellied and patterned like Aboriginal paintings, with circles, dots and waves.

You look up at the vampiric Aboriginal creation, the Yara Ma Yha Who. This monster will, if you stay under its tree, climb down – it's a fantastic climber but a terrible walker – and use the suckers on the ends of its limbs to drain the blood out of you. After a big drink from a nearby water hole, it will take a long nap. If the food – that's you – is still there when it wakes, it will open its hinged, toothless jaws and swallow you whole! To help digest you, it will perform a wild, rhythmic dance below the fig trees. It then naps again and on waking, regurgitates you like a slippery eel. Finally, Yara Ma Yha Who will poke you with a stick, but if you lie still, the monster will get bored and leave.

You will recover, eventually, but will notice you are slightly red in colour and hairless. If you linger too long under the fig tree though, the Yara Ma Yha Who will return and eat you again and again until you become one of them.

Yara Ma Yha Who is just one of many Aboriginal stories that have been told for 40,000 years, carrying the voices of the people and lessons on survival, belief and nature. The monsters in these tales are similar to other cautionary creations found around the world, which warn young ones not to stray, even in daylight.

If you do go out into the Australian forests, be careful, be cautious and look up!

MINOTAUR

OTHER NAMES Asterion

GREECE

Crouched down in the dark corner, his hands holding a flaming torch and a dagger, a man listens to the strange sounds that echo down the long, winding passages. Deep in the belly of this place he can hear the snorts, scrapes and roars of a beast. He stands, letting out a little more thread, his lifeline to find his way to freedom, as he moves along the snake-like paths of the Labyrinth. From above, you would see a tiny man lit by the glow of his torch, steadily moving to the centre of a maddening maze of walls. Once there, he will find a grotesque monster, part-man, part-bull, who is trapped forever in this puzzle prison: the Minotaur!

Theseus, the hero in this Greek legend, must meet this beast head on. He will fight for hours, and against all odds he will slay the creature, freeing the people of Athens from the Minotaur's terror. For years, the Athenian people have been sending the beast human sacrifices to stop its curse of plagues devouring their city.

The myth of the Minotaur can be seen in art, ceramics and sculptures throughout Greek history. His terrible temper and hunger drove a king named Minos to trap the Minotaur. The king asked Daedalus, an inventor, to design a place that no one could escape from, and he created the Labyrinth. But Theseus used a simple cotton thread to lead him back out, its simplicity was its brilliance!

Labyrinth? Maze? Which was the Minotaur trapped in? Labyrinths have a single path in, and a single path out. They are not as tricky as mazes, which have dead ends and lots of different pathways. It seems more likely the Minotaur was trapped in a sort of maze. This would explain how Theseus used a cotton thread to find his way out and why the Minotaur could not escape. The Minotaur is an incredible monster living within a puzzle, who has been infamous for around 2,500 years!

LOVELAND FROG

OTHER NAMES Loveland Frogman, Loveland Lizard

USA

The beautiful south-western town of Loveland, nicknamed 'Sweetheart of Ohio', in the USA, is famed for growing peaches and strawberries. It is also home to the infamous Loveland Frog!

Let's go back to the humid summer of 1955, cicadas clicking in the evening haze. A businessman is driving out of Loveland, nearing one of the town's many bridges that cross the Little Miami River. The light is fading and his headlights sweep past something on the bridge. There stands a fantastically freakish sight. Upright on leathery, hairless legs, a webbed hand held up to the headlights' glare, was a man frog! Panicked, the businessman sped away, but he would not be the only witness to the Loveland Frog.

In 1972, a local police officer saw a squat creature at the same location, frog-faced, lizard-like and standing on two legs. He stated later, 'I knew no one would believe me, so I shot it and put it in my car boot.'

In 2016, teenagers were out roaming alongside the Little Miami River when they photographed the Loveland Frog. The image was dark and grainy, but two large, glowing eyes on a large, human-sized shape can be seen in the black water.

This strange amphibious monster has hopped, squelched and walked the edges of Loveland for decades. Some say the town's regular flooding allowed the creature to grow so large. Nobody has captured a clear picture of it; the teenagers' photo was dark and blurred. Like most urban legends, the Loveland Frog is rarely photographed but widely talked about. Many say it's a hoax. In the end, the policeman's boot only contained a large pet iguana.

Have you ever heard frog calls by a lake, their loud rhythmic croaking? Imagine the sound a human-sized frog would make, and how high he could jump! The Loveland Frog is surely a hoax, but amphibians are incredible creatures that have inhabited our planet for millions of years. If you visit Ohio, drop in to Loveland, take a good camera, camp by the river and listen for the croaks ...

LUSCA

BAHAMAS

Have you ever wondered if the tide's continual movement – in and out; in and out – was made by something other than the Moon's gravity pulling on the oceans? Have you listened as the sea rises and falls and imagined it is breathing? What if it is? And what if it is actually the breath of a gigantic creature?

There are over one thousand mysterious blue holes surrounding the islands of the Bahamas, in the Caribbean. These blue holes are deep, mainly unexplored, and lead to underwater caves and tunnels. From above, they look like circular black holes in the ocean that contrast against the clear-blue tropical sea all around them. With dangerously strong currents and whirlpools, some divers and swimmers have died whilst exploring them.

Curled up in a blue hole off Andros Island is a phenomenal sea monster that has rightly inspired a series of *Sharktopus* movies – Lusca! This mega shark-octopus from Caribbean folklore has been sighted around the islands of the Bahamas and has apparently been attacking divers and swimmers for decades. It is between 23 and 60 metres long and has biting tentacles! It can change colour for camouflage, like smaller octopuses do, and sink to great depths onto the deep-sea floor.

In 1896, a decaying mass of blubber washed up in Florida, only a short boat ride north-west of the Bahamas. Was it Lusca? In January 2011, the head of a sea monster washed up on Grand Bahama Island, which was calculated to have come from a 10-metre-long body! But the body of what?

Scientists have blamed the sightings on giant squids or unusual water currents that make a monster shape seemingly appear in the blue holes. These plunging, mysterious holes are full of secrets, and scientists have discovered many unknown species of sea life in them. The soup of bacteria in the cave waters are similar to prehistoric seas. Perhaps Lusca has been down in its hole for 300 million years? Occasionally coming up for snacks!

GROOTSLANG

OTHER NAMES Groteslang

SOUTH AFRICA

Ingredients for making Grootslang, the South African Great Snake of the Orange River:

Diamonds – lots of precious, dazzling jewels created over billions of years in the Earth's mantle, just beneath its surface. You will need enough to encrust his cave walls and save two big ones for his eye sockets.

Mix in a double helping of greed and cleverness.

Next, add another sprinkling of greed and an appetite for eating humans.

Place in warm water in a cosy, deep cave. The Wonder Hole, a deep cave system in South Africa, is perfect.

To create the body, shape the monster to look like a 13-metre-long python. That's about the length of a bus.

Finally, add an elephant head and tusks, horns and fangs. And perhaps some legs if you're feeling creative. Some say add legs, some say no legs, it's just a matter of taste.

And *voilà*! You have just created Grootslang, which you may live to regret. Centuries of well-documented encounters with the greed-driven treasure-hunter Grootslang have earned it a place among monster legend. Ancient stories explain that Grootslangs were made by the gods, but they became too powerful, so they were split into parts, creating the very first elephants and snakes. Treasure-obsessed giant serpents, called leviathans, are common in mythology, reflecting humans' craving for treasure. In many monster myths, the selfish traits of people are represented by the monster to teach us how greed is vile and dangerous, especially when greed is wearing tusks and fangs!

If you are unlucky enough to meet Grootslang, if you just happen to stop by his deep cave in Richtersveld, he will eat you. Unless, yes there is an unless, you can bargain for your life by giving him gems. You have lots of diamonds, don't you?

JERSEY DEVIL

OTHER NAMES Leeds Devil

USA

You are deep in the New Jersey Pine Barrens of the USA. There is a strange calm within the tall cedar trees. The area is swampland that lies on an aquifer, a rock that holds on to water. The many streams that run through the trees around you are blood-red, and the shadows here are long and sharp. You can hear your heart beating: ***thump, thump, thump***. The trees seem to tighten in around you. What time is it? You must have been walking for hours. You look at your watch, but it has stopped. Then you hear it. A scream. A blood-curdling, hairs-stand-up-on-your-neck type of scream! It echoes around every cedar trunk, rippling the blood-red stream water and returning to the mouth that made it! The Jersey Devil stands up ahead: 3 metres tall with huge, leathery, black wings, half-folded behind its back. It has horns on top of its goat-skull head, furry legs and huge clawed hands. The wings unfurl and spread out, as wide as a bus. It screams again. Whatever time your broken watch says, it's time to go! Run!

The Jersey Devil is one of the most sighted monsters on Earth. In 1909, he was spotted by hundreds of people, but the legend began in 1735. A woman named Old Mother Leeds had twelve children. When her thirteenth child was born it was said to be cursed with wings and a goat's face. Shortly after birth, it flew up the chimney and out into the Pine Barrens, where it still lives to this day. Gossip, superstition and a fear of witches that was common during the eighteenth century brought this creature to life.

Surely such a long-standing monster legend must have a basis in truth? Police posters stated that the Jersey Devil was a hoax, but the Philadelphia Zoo offered a $10,000 reward for its capture. The Jersey Devil remains at large!

LAGARFLJÓTSORMUR

OTHER NAMES Lagarfljót Worm

ICELAND

Iceland is an easily imagined birthplace of mythical beasts. A landscape of ice-covered volcanoes, glaciers, geysers and bubbling hot springs below a sky rippling with the Northern Lights. If you were a sea monster, this would be the place to live, a place well used to legends and epic sagas.

What do the following people have in common? The Head of the Icelandic National Forest Service, a class of schoolchildren and their teacher, a group of underwater cable engineers and the Icelandic Truth Commission. They have all seen evidence of the Lagarfljótsormur – or Lagarfljót Worm. They, and 700 years' worth of sightings, folklore and mystery surround the freshwater lake of Lagarfljót, near Egilsstaðir in Iceland.

In the deep lake lurks a giant, worm-like serpent. Longer than a tennis court, it breaks the ice-crusted surface with its many humps and coils. The Lagarfljót Worm moves quickly through the glacial waters, and in 2012, it was captured on film. Remarkably, this slithering beast also leaves the water and drapes itself in the trees that fringe the lake. It hangs over branches, like slippery Christmas tinsel, before dropping back into the depths.

But is the worm naughty or nice? The Icelandic Annals of 1345 describe it as 'A wonderful thing'. Yet, in the 1500s it was far from wonderful. The monster was blamed for the lake flooding the land and causing local tragedies. In 1862, the folktale of 'the heath worm and the gold' became popular. It tells of a young girl who kept a gold ring with a slug – a heath worm – which was meant to bring luck and riches. Both were kept in a box in a drawer, but within days the drawers were splintered as the monster grew. Out of control, both gold and slug were cast into the lake!

What's behind all the sightings? Is it methane gas bubbles breaking the surface, unearthing debris from the lakebed? Perhaps eels? Whatever it is, the sight of a giant worm in a Christmas tree is something we all want to witness.

BATIBAT

OTHER NAMES Bangungot

PHILIPPINES

You don't like to say anything, but you don't like the new flat-packed dining table. Juice has been spilt, the knives and forks are on the floor and the plates are cracked.

A lack of good table manners has been blamed on you, but you swear you are just sitting eating your food! There! A napkin slithers off the table, pulling a wine glass and salt pot with it! Why is the wood so lumpy?! And why is that knot of wood, that looks like a dark brown eye, staring at you? Where did you get this table from?!

In Filipino mythology, the Ilocano people believe that a nasty, vengeful monster lives in the trees. The Batibat, a bloated, heavy and horrifying old woman lurks in the branches. Do not cut down the Batibat's tree! If you do, say to make the foundations for a wooden house, you will take the Batibat with you. Unseen, she squeezes into the wood, and once it is installed in the house, so too is the Batibat, and her vile behaviour will soon claim victims.

If you dare to sleep above the wood she hides in, she will emerge from it at night, like a giant weevil, fully reforming into her hideous, fleshy mass. Then she will crush the sleeper whilst giving them awful nightmares! Batibat's other name is Bangungot, and this word is also used to describe a disease that causes death while people sleep. Batibat seems to have been created to explain this frightening illness, before science could explain it.

So, if Batibat's tree was cut up and made into a nice dining table, you had better wriggle your toes and bite your nails all night, as that is the only way to deter her attacks. Or a trip to the recycling centre and eating off your lap would do it.

BEAST OF GÉVAUDAN

FRANCE

Can you imagine the terror that swept through Gévaudan, France in 1764, as one by one people were being savagely attacked by a monster in the woods? Wolves killed thousands of people in Europe during the eighteenth century, but this was different. Survivors, and there were few among the hundreds of attacks, stuttered out the following awful details – twice the size of a wolf, orange-coloured fur, black streak along the back, long muzzle with huge fangs, fluffy end to the tail and skin so tough that bullets bounce off it. That does not sound like a normal wolf.

These ferocious people-eating attacks continued, and after a year the King of France, Louis XV, sent in the dragoons – armed military men – to hunt the beast. But still the attacks continued for years. Next, expert animal trackers arrived and they killed a large wolf. People celebrated the slaying of the Beast of Gévaudan, but their joy was soon cut short. The attacks continued and hysteria quickly spread. People were being eaten whilst tending cattle. Nobody felt safe.

A man called Jean Chastel eventually hunted down the huge animal. Using a silver bullet in his pistol, he shot and killed the beast. A large wolf was stuffed and even displayed at the court of King Louis XV, and crowds thought it was the famous Beast. But what was it? An autopsy investigated the dead body and found that it appeared to be wolf-like but was much larger, with longer teeth, red eyes and strange eyelids. Was it a werewolf? Or perhaps a prehistoric creature? The descriptions of the Gévaudan 'wolf' are very similar to the ancient and extinct ankalagon, a bear-sized animal with a long face, orangish fur, a long tail and teeth. Could the Beast of Gévaudan have survived 66 million years? It would explain why it was so hungry after such a long time!

MORBACH MONSTER

OTHER NAMES Werewolf of Morbach

GERMANY

Are you scared of the dark? Light seems to drive away fear. Even a single candle can make you feel protected. It certainly does if you live in the Morbach region of south-west Germany. The power of a single, lit candle has supposedly protected a town for more than 200 years against a murderous monster ...

The story goes that in 1988, a group of officers from the Hahn Air Base were returning from a night out in Wittlich, a town in the Morbach area. As they reached the crossroads, they noticed the small, stone, candle-lit shrine was in darkness, no longer burning. The candle was always alight. They started joking around, 'It's coming!' they shouted. Howling and laughing they returned to base. That candle was never allowed to go out. Keep the light lit, the monster will not come. Blow the light out ...

The night was calm but not for long. An alarm was triggered on the 4-metre fence surrounding the air base. A security officer went to investigate, shining his torch he saw something unimaginable! A menacing, 3-metre-tall, wolf-like creature was standing on hind legs, with its huge mouth open and blood-red eyes. Suddenly, it leapt over the fence and vanished. Search dogs came, but they whimpered and refused to follow the scent trail left by the beast.

The Morbach Monster first terrorised the town in 1810, when it was shot and wounded by villagers and the candle was originally lit to ward off the werewolf curse. After that night in 1988, the candle was immediately relit, and the werewolf has not been seen since.

Werewolf transformations are the stuff of nightmares. Skin stretching, muscles tearing, claws growing through fingertips, hair smothering arched backs, fangs cutting through human gums that fill long muzzles. After being bitten or cursed, people change into wolves on the full moon. A silver bullet will kill them, or in the case of the Morbach Monster, light a small candle to dispel the darkness and keep them at bay.

LOCH NESS MONSTER

OTHER NAMES Nessie, Niseag

SCOTLAND

'Welcome on board the Loch Ness Tour. For safety, please do not feed the monster, and in the event of an emergency, put on life jackets.' The boat moves over the black water as the rain-heavy clouds overhead threaten thunder. The passengers are buzzing with excitement, sporting 'Nessie' hats and T-shirts, their cameras ready to catch a glimpse of Scotland's famed Loch Ness Monster.

The boat circles over the centre of the loch, which is 230 metres deep. You feel a drop of rain, and within seconds the loch is hammered with a downpour. You watch the boat's rippling wake. A dark shape is following the boat at speed, maybe a shoal of fish? Then what looks like a smooth grey cable breaks the surface, then another rises up and a third! You say out loud, but your voice is lost against the engine sound, 'It's Nessie!' But everyone's inside, sheltering from the rain. Next, the sea monster raises its head as the sun emerges from the black storm clouds and illuminates the ancient features of the Loch Ness Monster, before it slowly sinks back to the deep.

You buy a Nessie keyring. Not that you will ever need reminding of the day you saw the Loch Ness Monster! You are one of the lucky ones to have spotted this shy giant.

From 1870 up to present day, the mystery of the Loch Ness Monster has bewitched and obsessed people. There have been numerous sightings, photographs, films and scientific research carried out, but there's no accepted proof that it exists. Most accounts are hoaxes; toy submarines, inflatables, digital trickery or mistakenly identified logs, swimming animals or seaweed. Is it an extinct plesiosaur left over from the Cretaceous Period? Doubtful, as the loch is only 10,000 years old and was previously frozen for 20,000 years! Perhaps it's a massive eel. Moray eels can grow 4 metres long. Whatever Nessie is, she is adored across the globe.

MOTHMAN

USA

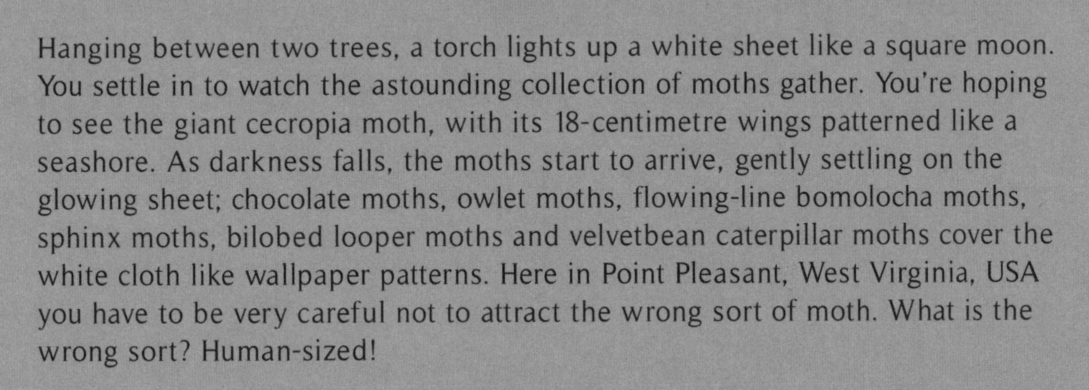

Hanging between two trees, a torch lights up a white sheet like a square moon. You settle in to watch the astounding collection of moths gather. You're hoping to see the giant cecropia moth, with its 18-centimetre wings patterned like a seashore. As darkness falls, the moths start to arrive, gently settling on the glowing sheet; chocolate moths, owlet moths, flowing-line bomolocha moths, sphinx moths, bilobed looper moths and velvetbean caterpillar moths cover the white cloth like wallpaper patterns. Here in Point Pleasant, West Virginia, USA you have to be very careful not to attract the wrong sort of moth. What is the wrong sort? Human-sized!

Between 1966 and 1967, the night sky held a terrible secret, one that all who saw it will never forget. Grave diggers working at night saw a human-sized creature with large wings fly over them and disappear into the trees. Couples travelling home reported a large flying man with a 3-metre wingspan and glowing red eyes illuminated in their car headlights. A fireman reported seeing a huge red-eyed bird, and locals also spotted the black shape of the Mothman above them during that time. Newspapers across the country carried stories of these monster sightings, and the mystery became a celebrated event.

Then a tragedy struck thc town. The well-used Silver Bridge collapsed, killing many people, and the Mothman became a symbol for death. This idea travelled across the world as far as Russia, where sightings of the Mothman were reported before tragic events happened.

But rather than run from this mysterious creature, Point Pleasant welcomes the mystery that attracts visitors to their town. A 4-metre metallic statue of the Mothman stands in the town centre, and each year, the Mothman Festival celebrates this strange insect with a pancake-eating competition! Twelve thousand visitors attend the festival, hoping for a glimpse of the mammoth moth.

Scientists, however, believe it was a sandhill crane that originally flew over Point Pleasant; red-ringed eyes and a 2-metre wingspan. What do you think? Well, something heavy just knocked your bug sheet down!

ANTARCTICA

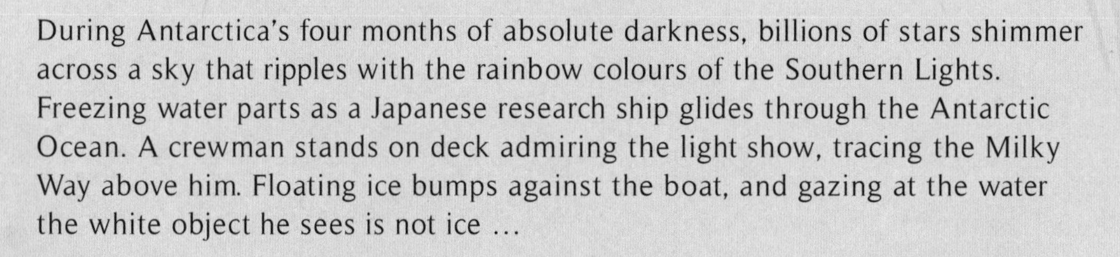

During Antarctica's four months of absolute darkness, billions of stars shimmer across a sky that ripples with the rainbow colours of the Southern Lights. Freezing water parts as a Japanese research ship glides through the Antarctic Ocean. A crewman stands on deck admiring the light show, tracing the Milky Way above him. Floating ice bumps against the boat, and gazing at the water the white object he sees is not ice ...

A haunting shape, like a giant ghost, is rising up. It's at least 30 metres long, much longer than the research ship. A submarine? Out here? As the shape surfaces, it reveals a huge body with long arms. Two circular, black eyes look straight at the man who stares, frozen. The cold starts to burn his wide-open eyes. Then the giant white monster slowly sinks back into the frozen sea, leaving only the rainbow sky reflecting off the empty wet expanse.

Ningen, meaning 'human' in Japanese, was first sighted by a Japanese research ship in the 1990s. It was shared on the Internet and ever since, there have been a large number of sightings of this gentle but vast sea monster. Google Images were shared showing a white, human-like creature in the sea, and many hoax photos exist of Ningens walking on the Antarctic ice.

But what could it be? The sea seems the most natural home to any monster, it has depths we struggle to imagine and animals so strange that they put monsters to shame. Could the sightings be a pod of beluga whales? They are pale and smooth with black eyes. Or white albino rays or skates that blend with the ice? Perhaps it was an abyssal cusk eel or hadal snailfish, strange creatures that live in the abyssal plain in the deep sea. With its human features, perhaps the Ningen is a mix of mermaid and ghost, or maybe it's an undiscovered sea creature, a very gentle monster of the deep.

CHONCHON

OTHER NAMES Chaihue, Chuchu, Chuncho

ARGENTINA AND CHILE

Before we begin, try to remember the phrase, 'Come back tomorrow for some salt.' You will need it.

It is a moonless night; you have thrown open the windows as the temperature is mild and there's a light breeze. A dog barks some way down the road and cats are meowing around the bins when another sound joins in.

Tué, tué, tué!

It's an odd screechy noise, not unlike an owl, but there is something about it, as if a person is pretending to make owl noises. There it goes again … ***Tué, tué, tué!*** Looking up you cannot see anything, so you go to bed. In southern Chile and south-west Argentina that sound can only mean one thing – Chonchon! You don't know it yet, but you are in for a rough night …

Can you hear the sound of wings flapping? There! Hovering in your window is a shocking sight, an absurd sight! A human head, but the ears have turned into two huge wings. It has feathers as hair, talons on its bird feet and razor-sharp teeth to suck your blood! ***Flap flap flap***, the vile Chonchon screeches its sound again, ***Tué, tué, tué!*** as it goes for your neck. Now say it! 'Come back tomorrow for some salt!'

The Chonchon frowns, flaps and flusters and flies away! Phew. Tomorrow someone will knock on your door and awkwardly ask for salt. You will be face to face with the evil Kalku, or wizard, who turned into the Chonchon. How did the Kalku remove its head? It rubbed magic cream around its neck, and its head flew off to find blood and cast curses.

If anyone had found the Kalku's headless body, they could have rolled it on its tummy to stop the head from reattaching.

Japan's Nukekubi monster also detaches its head to drink blood at night, before rejoining its body again and living a normal life! If you have any other ideas on how to survive a Chonchon, we're all ears!

FUTAKUCHI-ONNA

OTHER NAMES Two-Mouthed Woman

JAPAN

There are a wild array of monsters in Japanese folklore. Tenjōnami is funny, Nuppeppō is absurd, Ikuji is magnificent and Futakuchi-Onna is horrifying. But they all have one thing in common: they carry a message, warning or threat.

You would know if you met a monster, wouldn't you? Especially if it was right in front of your eyes ...?

How lovely, you are invited to a traditional Japanese home for lunch with the kind host, a quietly spoken lady who has prepared green tea, a bowl full of rice balls and sushi. Kneeling at the low table, the lady quietly encourages you to eat and drink.

'Are you eating?' you ask as you tuck into a rice ball. 'No, I'm not hungry,' she smiles. The rice ball is yummy, you reach for another and notice that the bowl is almost empty, how strange. The host looks peacefully at you, 'Try some sushi?' Then you hear another voice screech ... 'That sushi is mine!' You stare at the lady, but she just smiles and nods for you to keep eating. You nervously reach for the last rice ball when a black slither of hair grabs it from your hand and whips it away. Then another snake of hair forms fingers, grabs the rest of the sushi and disappears behind the lady's back. Slowly, she turns her head, her hair parts and reveals a grotesque open mouth stuffed with food that the hair has fed to it. All the while, the mouth is hissing rude words! You've lost your appetite.

The Futakuchi-Onna, or two-mouthed woman, looks like a normal woman, but she has a secret. A hidden monster mouth that is greedy, rude and nothing like the kind host's personality. Horror heads are common in Japanese monsters: Rokurokubi is a head on a long ribbon neck, and Nukekubi's head detaches and flies around. These monsters were the result of curses or punishments on mean and greedy people. For over 500 years, Japan has been overrun with these badly behaved oddities. Hair-raising!

GOLD-DIGGING ANTS

OTHER NAMES Giant Ants

PAKISTAN

'Gold! Gold!' The shouts echo around the dusty Deosai Plateau in Pakistan. The sun lights up the shimmering grains on the surface. It's gold, glittering and mesmerising. Gold that has been present on Earth since 3.8 billion years ago. Precious, made into jewellery, coins, components in industry and medicine. As the gold hunters stare at the radiant soil, an army of shadows darken the ground! ANTS! Not tiny ants that carry leaves, not even the larger ants that can bite, but ants the size of foxes, or some say even bigger, furry and moving fast. Here come the legion of Gold-Digging Ants!

The legend of the Gold-Digging Ants has flourished thanks to two men visiting the region thousands of years ago. Herodotus, a Greek historian and Pliny the Elder, a Roman author, both travelled to the Deosai Plateau 300 years apart and wrote about their experiences there. Their writings included notes about these insect giants who roamed the plateau. They described them as helpful, digging burrows and unearthing gold dust.

Huge furry ants digging up gold dust for people to collect, does this seem believable? Long before the arrival of Pliny the Elder and Herodotus, the Persian-speaking Minaro people lived on the plateau. They spoke of the mus kuhi – the marmot, which is a large ground squirrel – who helpfully dug up gold when burrowing. But non-Persian visitors, even famous Roman and Greek ones, can struggle with pronouncing words in a new language. They heard '*mur kuh*' when in fact the Minaro said '*mus kuhi*'. '*Mur kuh*' is Persian for mountain ant!

Could a monster be born from a translation mistake!? Simply by hearing mountain ant, not marmot? A translation monster creation, don't you think that's wonderful? A simple pronunciation mistake, repeated over time, created the mythological Gold-Digging Ants! It does make you wonder how many other monsters are just mistaken words for simple things.

BISHOP-FISH

OTHER NAMES Sea Monk

POLAND

'Open the doors!' the guards commanded, letting the fisherman run through the ornate halls, saltwater trailing behind him onto the marble floors. 'Quick!' the fisherman called as he supported the large net in his arms. The creature inside looked around, its mouth bubbling as it was bumped and jostled.

The fisherman nervously bowed when he was brought before the King of Poland. The creature peered through the net at the king, dripping and flapping and struggling to breathe.

Everyone looked into the net and gasped as the creature seemed to sit up, blink at the king, bow and raise what looked like a hand to make the sign of the cross. 'Release me, please. *Puść mnie, proszę.*' It then smiled a sad smile.

The king's eyes softened, 'It looks like a bishop! Look at its robes, and it made the holy sign. Release it as it wishes!'

The Bishop-Fish was rushed from the palace straight to the seashore, where it was released. On hitting the water, it apparently raised its fin-hand again and disappeared beneath the waves.

In the 1500s there was nothing fantastical about the Bishop-Fish. It was featured in *Historiae Animalium* in 1558, a book of REAL animals. The illustration made the Bishop-Fish look like a monk giving a blessing. Tales of these odd religious lookalikes strengthened people's belief in miracles and in the church. But what was this sad creature? Surely not a bishop who lived in the oceans? On closer inspection it would appear to be a squid, ray or angel shark specimen.

Humans like to see faces in things that are not human. This is called pareidolia and explains lots of strange things that we think of as half-human, half-animal. It can benefit the animal, too. The Japanese samurai crab has a shell pattern that resembles a samurai warrior, so the fishing community throw it back and will not eat it out of respect! It can be a clever adaptation for survival. The Bishop-Fish had a lucky escape.

OWLMAN

OTHER NAMES Cowanden

ENGLAND

The place: St Mawnan and St Stephen's Church in Cornwall, in south-west England. The date: 17 April 1976. Why are we here, time-travelling back to flared trousers and cape-wearing days? We are here to witness a monster sighting that catapulted this creature into fame and Cornish folklore.

A family on a holiday are enjoying the lovely warm April weather. Their girls, aged nine and twelve, are exploring the village of Mawnan when they see something so monstrous that the family packs up and ends their holiday! Looking up, over the church tower, the girls spot a large bird shape against the sky. With wide-open wings, it has the body of a man, glowing red eyes and it's hissing. Terrified, the girls run. Their sketch of the 'Owlman of Mawnan' showed a huge, feathered man with pincers for hands. Pamphlets were printed in Cornwall entitled *The Monster of Falmouth Bay*, and the Owlman legend took off.

Fifty years earlier, two boys were chased by a birdman by the river in Mawnan! More sightings followed in the 1970s, '80s and in 1995, an American biologist was confronted by a giant, wide-mouthed, grey birdman. She described it as 'frightening' in a letter to the local paper.

Human-bird monsters are common in mythology; Alkonost and Sirin are bird women from Russia, Inmyeonjo is a Korean creature, Harpies come from Greek myths and Kinnara are from India.

But what could it be? The answer would seem to lie with owls. Seems obvious, but the Eurasian eagle owl – bubo bubo – has a wingspan of almost 2 metres! It has long ear tufts and striking orange eyes that seem to glow among the dark feathers. It is one of the largest owl species and, in flight, it could resemble the Owlman. There are no photos of him and some people say the reports are hoaxes. Despite this, thc addition of a mythical monster to an area of outstanding natural beauty can only enhance the visitor experience!

OX-HEAD AND HORSE-FACE

OTHER NAMES Gozu and Mezu

CHINA

Scooby Doo and Shaggy, fish and chips, Batman and Robin, sweet and sour, hugs and kisses. These are all strong double acts, but they have nothing on the visual impact of the two Chinese mythical guardians Ox-Head and Horse-Face!

Their names leave nothing to the imagination. They have large, human bodies, with the dead heads of an ox and a horse attached. They may sound like a double act, but their jobs couldn't be any darker or crueller. These beasts are the guardians of the underworld, the place you go after death. They are the first beings you meet on your way to hell, known in ancient Chinese mythology as Diyu. The judge, King Yama, looks at the life you have led and decides whether to let you through unharmed or punish you. Originally overworked and badly treated animals, Ox-Head and Horse-Face were pitied by King Yama and became his court attendants, security guards, receptionists, policemen and torturers! They seem to enjoy multitasking in their role of making people pay for their sinful lives. Using spikes and hammers, they will carry out terrible punishments on anyone King Yama demands them to, smiling as they work!

These ancient guardians are part of the images of hell in China. They feature in the Hell Scrolls and in an epic work of ancient Chinese literature called *Journey to the West*. In the story, the Monkey King, Sun Wukong, is chased by Ox-Head and Horse-Face for tricking them and escaping hell. Ox-Head and Horse-Face are big and brutish, but they are not clever. Sun Wukong goes on a fantastic journey until he eventually gets back to hell and removes his name and all monkeys' names from the death register.

These two monsters would look good on a movie poster, wearing leather jackets or jumping over burning cars. Instead, they are waiting to welcome you into hell …

GULYABANI

TURKEY

Bang. Bang. Bang. Someone is knocking at the window in the dead of night. The Turkish town of Sakarya is being terrorised. In the summer of 2014, residents hear constant knocking on their windows and doors. For eighteen months this sound has woken them from their sleep, but when they search, all they glimpse is a tall, ghoulish figure. Exhausted, the townspeople set up night watches, desperate to catch the monster. The local police even interview the residents, asking them what they saw. They all gasp, 'Gulyabani!'

Gulyabani, monster of the desert, lurks in silent places. He rests in cemeteries by day and rises to haunt lone travellers, townsfolk and naughty children by night. He is described as a towering ghoul with a beard as long as his robes, and the stench of death follows him like a shadow. His long, sharp nails scratch rooftops and his fists bang on windows, sending people mad with fear. If you looked out of the window in the night, Gulyabani would be lurching over rooftops, his beard and robes dragging over buildings, the reek of his ghoulish body killing plants.

Gulyabani is a monster from Turkish folklore, but he seems to have different characteristics in different areas. He can be a female ghoul with backwards-facing feet or an old wasted man with a long stick and a sickly, strange smile. Sometimes he eats people, other times he scares them to death. If children are naughty then he takes them, and he has been used in many households to scare children into going to sleep. Not the nicest bedtime story!

Famous enough to star in films as a puppet on stilts, looming over and lunging at the screaming characters, he is part of ancient folklore. But he is still as popular today as centuries ago.

Beware of Gulyabani, monster of the sands, he'll come knocking with his sharp, clawed hands. Always lock your windows, go check your doors, or the Gulyabani monster will grab you in his jaws!

BULGASARI

OTHER NAMES The Can't Kill

KOREA

'It cannot be killed,' cried the monk. 'It cannot be killed, no matter what you do. That is why we call it Bulgasari! The Can't Kill!'

The Korean monks of the Goryeo kingdom created Bulgasari, who grew from just a tiny bug that nibbled on needles and chopsticks and snacked on scissors and nails. For lunch, he had garden forks and hoes, and then he grew and grew and changed ...

Bulgasari transformed into a fearsome mixture of impressive beasts: body of a bear, nose of an elephant, rhinoceros' eyes, tail of a cow, tiger's legs and fur made of needles. His legs made him run as fast as the wind; his fur was an armour that was impossible to pierce. Sharp eyes and a huge body made him dangerous and cunning. And his main food of choice? Iron. He ate iron like we might eat puddings. Tearing up train tracks, fences, gutters and pipes.

But soon he became a problem. Bulgasari was created by monks to defend them, but he soon proved to be a far bigger threat. The monks tried to kill him, but he had eaten so much iron that he was invincible! They set fire to him, thinking he would burn, but he just ran around wearing the fire like a cloak, setting all the houses in the town alight! He was left unharmed ...

There are many versions of Bulgasari in Korean folklore, and in each version he cannot be killed. In modern versions, he is seen as a protector against fire, illness and political power. His resilience and fireproof skills are considered lucky, and his images are placed on buildings to ward off fire. Bulgasari is also a story of greed, as his constant hunger for iron was impossible to quench. The legend of Bulgasari has even appeared on the big screen in the first North Korean film to feature special effects. He's Korea's own Godzilla.

HERENSUGE

OTHER NAMES Erensuge, Lerensuge

SPAIN

Along the Pyrenees mountain range that rises up along the French-Spanish border, within the mythical deep abyss of Aralar, lies a giant, scaled dragon of Basque mythology. Listen carefully, can you hear her shrieking call? It's as if her voice is split; it's not one sound but a chorus of voices. That is because Herensuge doesn't have just one fanged, serpent-like head but seven! This seven-headed dragon, very much like the Greek monster Hydra, is the villain in many stories of heroic heroes slaying a dragon.

Each one of Herensuge's seven heads are said to be her children. When they grow large enough, the heads fall off and grow into another separate and fully formed Herensuge. Let's do some maths: if seven children grow seven more heads, and then each of those children go on to make seven more children, in only three generations you would have 16,807 Herensuges! The sky would be full of them, like flocks of vicious, biting starlings, soaring over the mountains, their wing tips slicing off the tops of tall trees. What to feed this large, hungry family? People, lots of people, who they carry off into their caverns to feed on. It's their version of doing the big family supermarket shop.

Stories of Herensuge and other mythical dragons appear in most cultures. People genuinely believed in their existence. Legends and tales, such as 'The Grateful Tartalo and the Herensuge', were shared and recorded in old manuscripts. People never stopped watching the skies for the sound of leathery wings and the glint of massive talons.

Dragon monsters are one of the most popular creatures, still adored by thousands. They appear in films, books and television shows, such as *Harry Potter* and *The Hobbit*. There is no account that Herensuge sat atop a pile of glittering gems, like the famous Smaug from *The Hobbit*. She was too busy hunting for enough food to feed seven hungry serpent mouths.

PESANTA

SPAIN

Catalonia, a beautiful region in north-east Spain, is home to a nightmare creature. You will never catch sight of it, maybe just a glimpse of a fast-moving darkness across the bedroom wall.

The warm night breeze billows the curtains as a sleeper enters into a deep, dreamless rest. The room is dark, but there is a sound … metallic scratching on the tiled floor. The sleeper wakes in a sweat, chest heavy as lead and their mind filled with vivid monstrous nightmares. They are sure that something was sat on their chest, filling their mind with awful fears. But the room is empty, there's just the warm breeze and black fur on the sheet!

They were visited by Pesanta. A huge black dog with steel paws. He enters the bedroom through small gaps in the dead of night to sit heavily on the chest of people sleeping. He fills their minds with nightmares, freezing their bodies like a statue.

Do you think that you are safe from his night terror, just because you do not live in Catalonia? Don't breathe a sigh of relief just yet. There are sleep monsters across the globe. Most countries have them: Night Hags and Night-Mares bring bad dreams and take your breath away.

These monsters of the night were created to explain sleep problems and mysterious illnesses before scientists could scan our brains and record our breathing.

Pesanta and other canine monsters are wonderfully popular in folklore because, even though dogs have been our companions for centuries, our ancestors would have feared wolves and wild dogs as predators. Many of these fears are funnelled into these terrifying monster dogs, such as Carbunclo, Fenrir, Grim and Penghou.

How can you protect yourself from Pesanta? Bars on your windows? Install an alarm system? No, just scatter millet seed around your bedroom and place a broom next to your bed, as Catalan legend instructs. That should do it.

So good night. Sleep well, if you can …

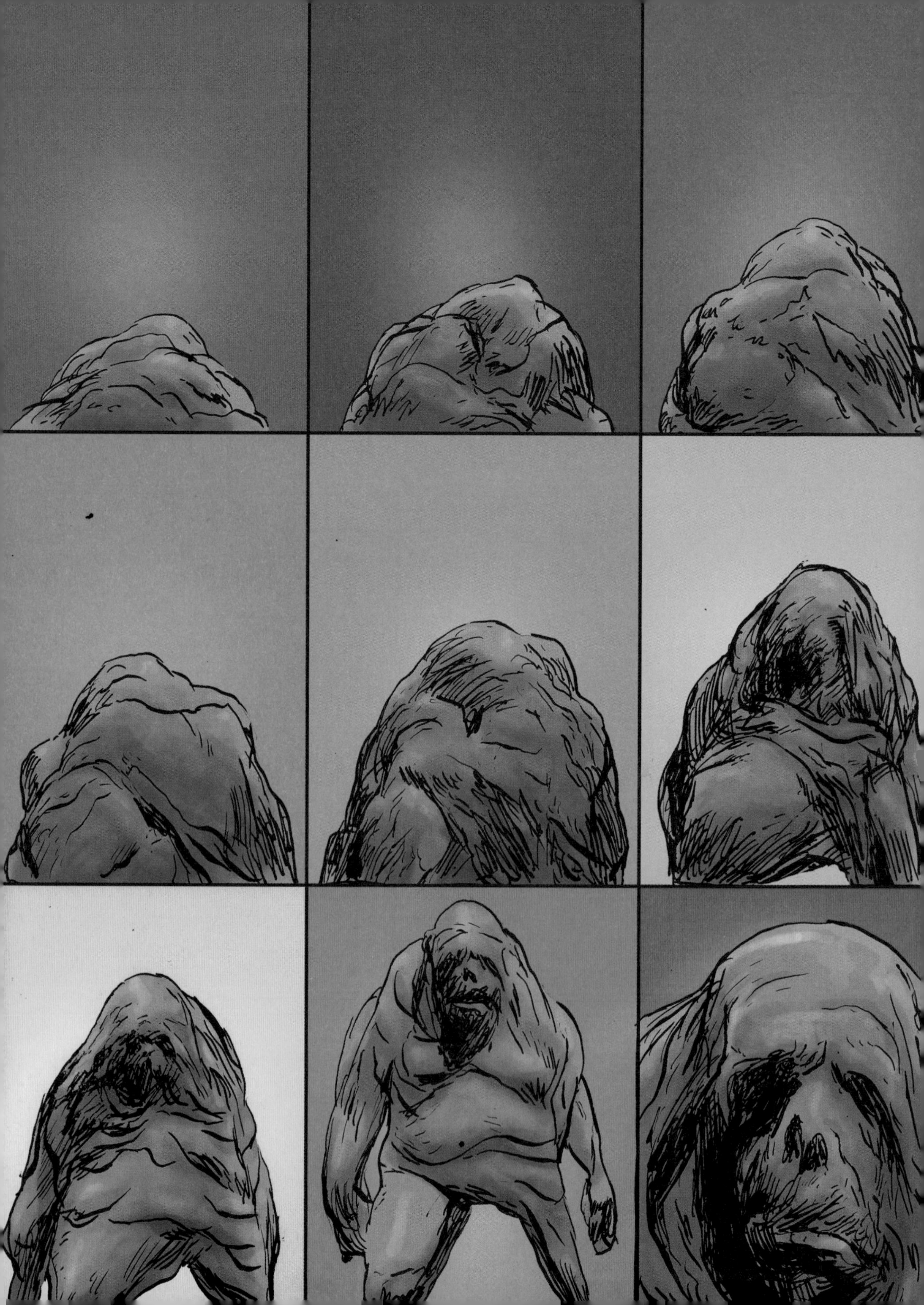

GOLEM

CZECH REPUBLIC AND ISRAEL

Mud; glorious, squelching, sticky stuff that you can jump into, roll in and make mud pies with. Clay; heavy, mouldable and smooth, which makes sculptures, roof tiles and pipes. These messy ingredients are perfect for making a Golem.

Making a Golem is simple (although we do not recommend it): roughly sculpt a figure from clay or mud, then write special Hebrew words on its forehead so you can control it. Have a clear idea of what you want your Golem to do, and be prepared for the monster to become uncontrollable and dangerous. The lesson to learn with selfishly created monsters is that they will always malfunction.

Mentioned in the Bible, Golem is a monster from Jewish folklore. Its name translates as 'shapeless thing', and it represents stupidity and thoughtlessness. One Golem story, among so many from Europe and the Middle East, is the Prague Golem. During the sixteenth century, in the stunning Czech Republic city of Prague, Rabbi Bezalel gathered clay from the banks of the Vltava river. Carefully, he moulded the heaps of heavy clay and slowly it began to take the shape of a person. The rabbi scratched words on the sticky forehead and immediately it awoke. At the rabbi's bidding, it began protecting the Jewish people in the city who had been treated badly. Golem, the monstrous bodyguard, with no thoughts of its own, just obeyed the rabbi's orders. But soon it grew, damaging property and hurting people accidentally. Bigger and bigger it grew, until it became a greater threat to the people it was meant to be protecting. The rabbi crept up to Golem and rubbed the words off its head, and the monster returned to being just a clay statue. The statue was thrown in the synagogue's attic, the door locked and the stairs removed so it could never be brought back to life. Centuries later, people investigated the locked attic looking for the mythical Golem, but they only found dust.

KELPIE

OTHER NAMES Nykk

SCOTLAND

The Scottish loch stretches out below the wild mountains; reeds pierce the mist at the water's edge. Eerily silent, most of the loch is cloaked in darkness. Along the shore walks a rambler, weary, hungry and dreaming of a warm bed, warm socks and warm soup. She looks towards the loch; Scotland is scattered with these deep, beautiful lakes. A whinnying sound breaks the silence. The woman looks around for horses, but there are none. The mist clears, and she notices a white horse with a dripping-wet mane on the shore. The horse moves towards her. She loves horses and appreciates the company. Approaching, with steam rising from velvety nostrils, the horse seems friendly. The horse's coat shines in the moonlight, and the woman reaches forwards to pat its soft neck. Her hand becomes stuck. Stuck like glue. The horse stares at the rambler, its eyes are tinged red. Suddenly, with one flick, the rambler is thrown onto the horse's back and it rides straight into the deep, freezing loch. A few bubbles rise to the surface ...

Kelpies are Scottish water horses who lure people into riding them, only to drown them. They possess the strength of ten horses and can shapeshift into beautiful, singing women or hairy men who crush their victims! Kelpies are a warning not to be tempted by the unknown.

There are Kelpie myths for almost every waterway in Scotland, each with their own sightings and superstitions. The myths say that if you can steal the bridle of the Kelpie then you will control it. But who dares go close enough to try?

To see Kelpies up close you don't have to wait on the edge of a loch. The sculptor Andy Scott created two 30-metre-high horse-head statues called 'The Kelpies' in 2014 that tower over the Forth river and Clyde canal in Falkirk, Scotland. The statues celebrate these legends of the water for their strength, danger and beauty.

ZOMBIE

OTHER NAMES Zombi, Zonbi

WORLDWIDE

What do you think of when you think about Zombies? Is it their rotting flesh, milky eyes, gnashing mouth and grasping hands? Or does their groaning, lurching walk and endless hunger come to mind? Hunger is all that's on a Zombie's mind. They're hungry for brains, guts and the rest of the body, too. Zombies are the superstars of the monster kingdom, which is surprising considering they have no charisma, nothing to say and are just eating machines who hang out in shopping centres. Despite this, Zombies have become a worldwide phenomenon.

But Zombies go back further than you might think. A 3,800-year-old clay tablet, from the ancient historic area of west Asia known as Mesopotamia, describes a poem that could be a line from a classic Zombie movie: 'I shall raise up the dead and they shall eat the living, and the dead shall outnumber the living.'

Zombies have been terrorising humans for thousands of years. But they really hit the big time in the 1600s thanks to the voodoo Haitian witch doctors of the Caribbean. These witch doctors used trances to turn people into Zombies so they could control them. Because of this, Zombies became linked to voodoo, a religious belief which includes the performance of rituals and magic. Haitian Zombies started appearing in films and books and evolved into the Zombies we know and love today. Soon, these undead creatures had a film category all of their own! Always in herds, eating people and groaning, some Zombies learnt to run, which made them seem less ghoul-like and more intelligent. Before, it was like running from a hungry tortoise, now it was like running from a flesh-eating cheetah!

But there are real-life Zombies causing terror at this very moment – zombie ants! A fungus called *ophiocordyceps unilateralis* – try saying that fast five times – invades ants' bodies. The fungus controls the ant's body as it fills it, until a spore spike bursts from its head, releasing more spores to control even more Zombie ants. Monsters come in all shapes and sizes, even microscopic ones!

QUETZALCÓATL

MEXICO

Ahead looms the Temple of Quetzalcóatl. Behind is a courtyard, where 100,000 people crowded to worship this god of wind, air and knowledge. Across the courtyard are the temples of the moon and sun gods. Deep below runs a treasure-filled tunnel to the burial place of the temple's priests. These are the ancient ruins of the glorious city of Teotihuacán. They were once home to one of the longest-living civilisations on Earth, the Mayans, and then, from the fourteenth century, the Aztecs.

The Mayans worshipped a feathered serpent called Kukulcan. He was the god of the morning and evening star, now known as the planet Venus. The Aztecs named him Quetzalcóatl, meaning 'the serpent of precious feathers'. A fierce, open-mouthed snake with a headdress of feathers, Quetzalcóatl was one of four monumental figures worshipped by the Aztecs. These gods were responsible for nature's mysteries, such as what makes rain, and who moves the sun?

The pyramid-shaped temples in Teotihuacán are decorated with carved images of this ferocious serpent. A stone carving of him slithers down the temple steps that were once awash with human blood. Imagine the ceremonies in front of these buildings! Sacrifices were made to Quetzalcóatl and the other gods. The courtyards were also flooded with water, which appeared gold under the rising and setting sun. It would have been an incredible sight.

The tunnel below the temples runs as long as a football pitch and was discovered thanks to a sink hole opening up in 2003. It had been unseen for 1,800 years. A remote-controlled camera explored the cramped passage, showing heaped pottery, piles of human bones, a handmade landscape of mountains, fool's gold stars and mercury lakes that were still shining in the darkness! The temple above was built on nearly 650 skulls.

A dinosaur was even named after this Aztec god. Quetzalcoatlus was a 65-million-year-old pterosaur. With a 10-metre wingspan, it is one of the largest-known flying animals ever discovered! Both the real and mythical creatures must have been a terrifying spectacle to behold!

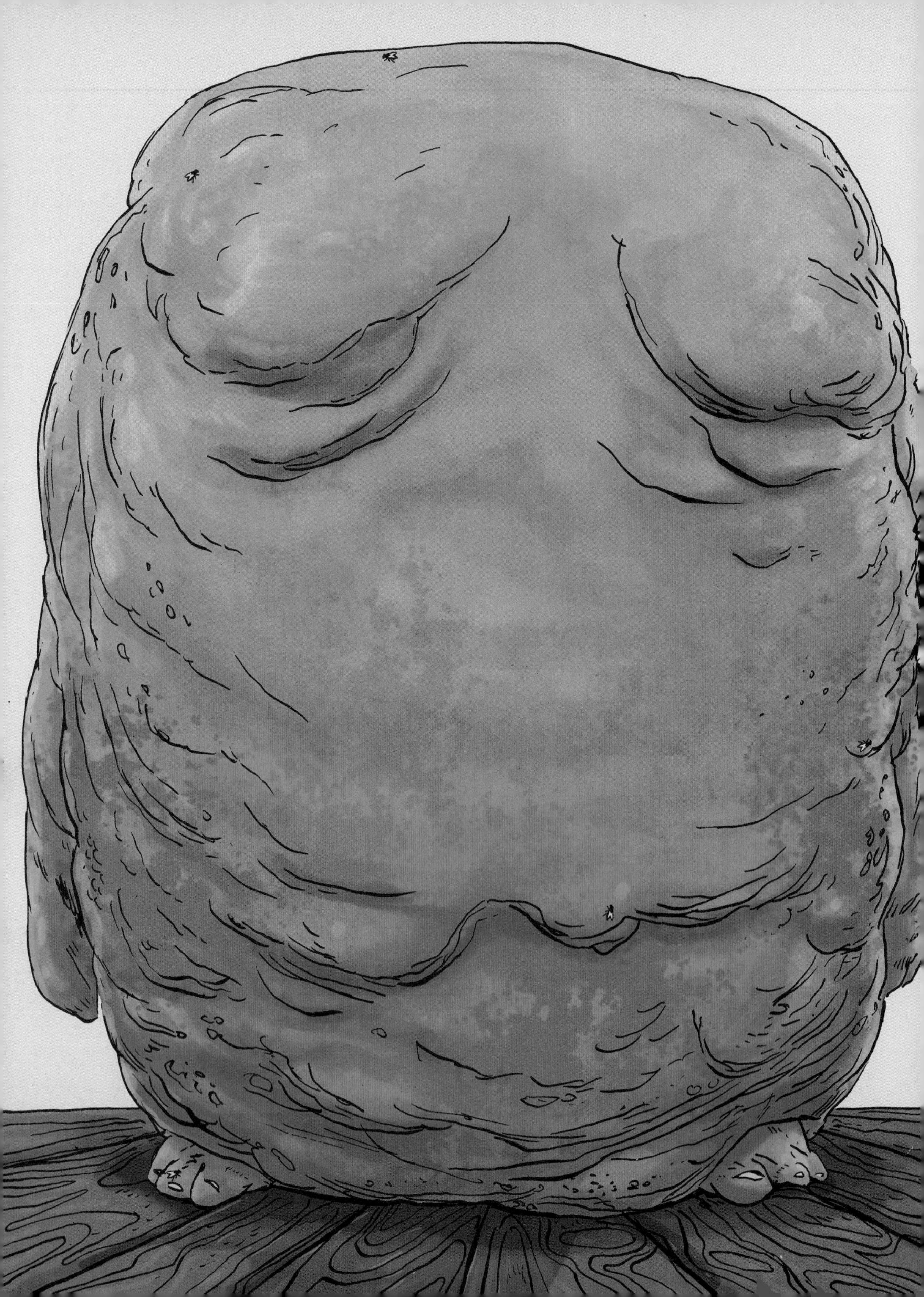

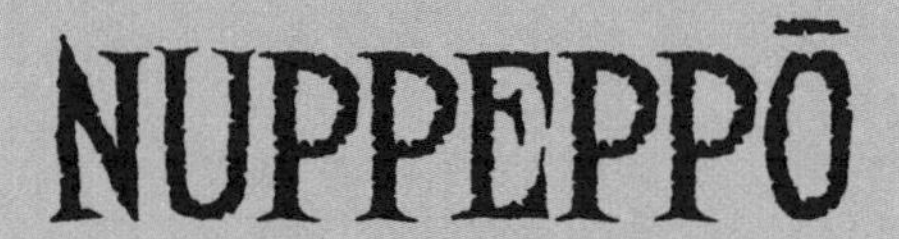

NUPPEPPŌ

OTHER NAMES Nuppefuhō

JAPAN

'What's for dinner tonight?'

'Nuppeppō and salad.'

Now, that is not a nice introduction to the Japanese monster Nuppeppō! Never introduce someone by placing them on the dinner table! But all will be explained, once you have been properly introduced ...

In the 1700s, which falls in the Edo period of Japanese history, a mysterious and odd creature began appearing in texts and illustrations. In one text, Shingo Zade Hōdai Mōgyū wrote:

'... it sucks the fat of the dead and eats to the fullest with a needle. In the past, they'd disguise as a doctor, but now they just come as Nuppeppō ...'

Nuppeppō is a big, greasy, oozing rotten-meat blob monster. A lonely blob with creases that make eyes of sorts and something like arms and feet. Sliding and creeping along empty streets in cities and towns, this monster hides in graveyards at night, scaring anyone who sees it. Or more precisely, anyone who smells it! Nuppeppō smells really bad, like eggs, rotting food, gas and poo. It is an innocent creature though, who does not want to be seen, but is pretty hard to miss. It wears white make-up, like the greasepaint clowns wear or the historical face whiteners of Japanese ladies, called geishas. In Japan, the white make-up shows that it is hiding its real personality. A 1.5-metre-tall meat slop wearing white make-up on an already dripping, creased face is a shocking sight. But it will not harm you, even though early writings say it gets fat from eating human fat from bodies, this is not how Nuppeppō is seen now.

But why is it on your dinner plate!? Apparently, if you can stand to eat a bit of a Nuppeppō, just a little nibble of the blob, you will be granted eternal life or eternal youth. Nobody is sure which, as the smell is so terrible it has never been eaten. Hold your nose and open your mouth, and let's see if the myth is true!

RAWHEAD AND BLOODY BONES

OTHER NAMES Blooddybones, Tommy Rawhead

ENGLAND AND USA

What do you keep in your wardrobe? What's stored under the stairs? Shoes? Old coats? Board games? Are you sure that's all there is in that cupboard in your room? Have you taken a closer look? Look through the keyhole, can you see into the dark corner, go on just take a peek? Is that a Halloween mask between the coats? What is that dripping sound? Just come closer, a little closer …

Drip drip, clatter, drip. Wheeze, drip, clatter, growl.

Rawhead and Bloody Bones is waiting. His red animal-skull head is slick with blood as he sits on a pile of white bones in the dark. He waits for someone to look at him. Just a peep through the keyhole is enough for him to see someone, lunge forwards and eat them!

Rawhead and Bloody Bones was born out of storytelling and legend in Lancashire, England. But his terrifying tale spread across the globe to settle in the USA, where he lurks in urban myths. Hungry, he crawls out of mountainsides after being disturbed and feasts on naughty children and cattle. His legend strikes fear into townsfolk, sending them running to lock up their livestock, their pets and children at night. The red-skulled predator will appear out of the shadows, leaving only a wet trail that leads back to his dark hole in the mountain.

Legends of skull-headed monsters, such as Rawhead and Bloody Bones, have lived on since the 1500s. They are made up of things that horrify and disgust people, including skulls of animals and hiding in the dark. Remember, these stories come from times when everything was lit by candlelight and there were lots of dark corners.

Rawhead and Bloody Bones is one of many monsters who delight in eating naughty children, a warning not to misbehave. Don't be too curious or Rawhead and Bloody Bones will find you and reward your curiousness! Listen …

Drip drip, clatter, drip. Wheeze, drip, clatter, growl. Aaaaaggghhhhhhhhhhh!

AMMIT

OTHER NAMES Ahemait, Ammut

EGYPT

Ammit, goddess, ferocious creature of ancient Egypt, was nicknamed the 'Devourer of the Dead' and 'Eater of Hearts'. Her huge, toothed grin and angry little eyes would be the last thing the wicked saw before she ate them. She represented a terrible fear for Egyptians: not passing from the living world into the afterlife ...

When an ancient Egyptian died, they journeyed from mummification to the afterlife, a kind of paradise after death. Their brain was hooked out of their nose and their soft, wet innards, including their precious heart, were stored in canopic jars. Sacred objects were buried with them to help their journey. Their souls were then led to the 'Hall of Two Truths', where several gods waited to meet them. Anubis, the jackal-headed god; Osiris, Lord of the Underworld; Thoth with the head of a bird; and the most terrifying of them all, Ammit. Created from Africa's ultimate predators, Ammit was part-lion, part-crocodile and part-hippo.

Crouched and hungry, Ammit stood drooling by the Scales of Justice, waiting for the dead to arrive. The gods judged how each Egyptian had lived their life. Their heart was placed on one side of the scales and on the other, they might hope for something heavy like a boulder. But instead, there was the 'Feather of Truth'. A single feather to weigh against all the bad and good inside their heart. The scales must balance. If not, the Egyptians had to convince the gods of their goodness and gift them amulets and spells to balance the scales.

Osiris and Thoth were fair, and if they accepted the gifts and excuses, the dead could pass into the afterlife. But if the dead had been sinful, or they had no offerings, Ammit grinned. The heavy heart would be judged 'not pure'. Anubis would throw their heart to Ammit, who'd catch it between her huge crocodile jaws, chew and swallow. Devoured, there was no afterlife for them.

JENNY GREENTEETH

OTHER NAMES Grindylow, Jinny Hewlett, Peg Powler

ENGLAND

The sun is low, casting long shadows on the emerald surface of the deep lake. Duckweed covers the water, like a blanket on a wet bed, suggesting a solidness, as if you could walk across the green carpet ...

But don't!

Can you see her? Look closer ... she's submerged just beneath the rippling weeds, waiting and hungry, like a foul, bloated fish. So still, so hungry, hiding until she can grasp the unsuspecting pond dipper. Long, slimy, weed-like hair and a grey, mottled, grinning face rise from the surface. Now out of the water, you see her long, clawing fingers and razor-sharp green teeth, like a pike's, opening and closing.

You've just come face-to-face with Jenny Greenteeth, a water hag. Jenny Greenteeth might live in water, but she can leave her dank, wet home and ooze out onto land, where she's known to hide in trees. So beware, quarries and dykes might look inviting on a hot summer's day, but Jenny could be waiting, ready to pull you under. After all, she was created by people as a warning to children and adults to protect them from drowning.

Jenny Greenteeth began as a local folklore story in northern England, but she hides behind different names depending on the area you visit. Grindylow, Jinny Hewlett and Peg Powler are all her different forms, and all are bad news for anyone who strays into her watery territory.

Jenny Greenteeth was the monster blamed for drownings and unexplained accidents in water, but perhaps she was misunderstood. She's a monster who was created to save lives. Wasn't she?

Wicked Jenny deep in the well, never look in and fall under her spell, she'll grab a hold and never let go, Wicked Jenny No, No, No ...

ALKONOST

RUSSIA

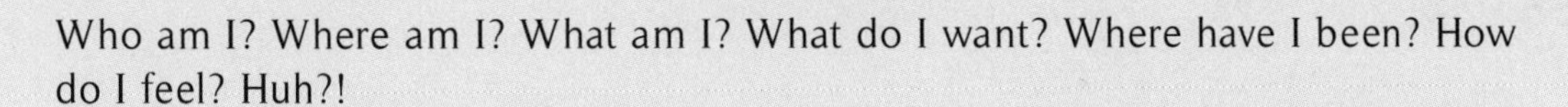

Who am I? Where am I? What am I? What do I want? Where have I been? How do I feel? Huh?!

The last thing you heard was a sweet melodic song, lilting, soft and achingly beautiful, coming from the treetops of this Russian woodland. A birdsong like no other. In parts it sounded like a woman singing, but then it shifted to the sound of songbirds, then back to the lullaby.

You have forgotten everything you ever knew and will not want for anything ever again, not food or sleep, not TV or even pets! But you are lucky, if you had been a bad person, then the lullaby would have caused you terrible pain and sadness.

You have been enchanted by the bird woman Alkonost. This creature has the head of a goddess, with beautiful human features, but where her neck joins her body, feathers appear, and her body is that of a large bird. Her bewitching song is powerful, and her giant eggs cause terrible thunderstorms when they roll into the sea.

Alkonost also has a sister called Sirin, who has the body of an owl. The pair are often mistaken for sirens, creatures who lure ships off course and bewitch people with song. But Alkonost's origins lie in an ancient Greek myth about humans transforming into birds. Her image was seen in religious texts from the tenth century.

There are so many bird women in mythology that they seem almost too common to fear; Gamayun is another Russian bird lady, Lilitu is from Mesopotamia, Harpies are found in Greece and Kinnara and Uchek Langmeidong are from India.

But to answer your questions; you are you, you are here, you are human, you want to read more monster stories, you have been in a Russian forest where you were put into a trance by a bird woman and you feel fantastic. There, all back to normal. Hang on, what is that beautiful song ...

MÃE-DO-OURO

OTHER NAMES Gold Mother

BRAZIL

Have you heard of St Elmo's Fire, Earthquake Lights or Min Min Lights? They are all types of unexplained, fiery, floating phenomena that intrigue scientists. Even ball lightning, a type of lightning that creates a sphere of electricity in the sky during storms, is not fully understood. When something is so rare that it is not well-recorded, or seems to act strangely, then people tend to think it is fake or supernatural.

The Mãe-do-Ouro is a huge fireball, but it also has the features of a woman. She moves across the Brazilian mountains, hovering over the ground where gold can be found. Her fiery, giant face can transform into a woman who wears a silken white dress with flaming hair. Generations of people in South America share stories of the time they saw the Gold Mother – another name for Mãe-do-Ouro – fly across the sky and over the mountains. The site that she rises from and returns to is marked with a large stone in São João del Rei, in south-east Brazil. Mãe-do-Ouro has been part of the folklore here since the mid-eighteenth century.

Does she remind you of something? She's a lot like our sun, rising and setting in the sky. Perhaps she is a way of explaining how the sun moves across the sky and sometimes appears as a huge red orb on the horizon. Finding ways to understand our awe-inspiring sun, before telescopes and star maps were common, must have given rise to legends.

Like the Mãe-do-Ouro, fiery balls appearing in the sky, and even inside buildings, have been popular mysteries for hundreds of years. Are they rare ball lightning, ghosts or another visual phenomenon? Could they be meteorites which regularly fall and strike the earth? Or could it be the Gold Mother showing you her treasures?

JENGLOT

INDONESIA

Settle down and listen to this chilling bedtime story: The Tale of the Hungry Doll.

'Bedtime!' Dad calls, 'Now!' The children reluctantly turn off the TV and head upstairs. In the hallway they pass their cat, who is crouched and hissing into a dark corner. 'The cat has a mouse again!' the children shout. The cat's eyes are wide, claws out.

In bed, the children finish reading their book about monsters when Mum shouts, 'Lights out'. 'But Mum, the cat is in here hissing!' Scooping up the angry cat, Mum kisses them goodnight and switches off the lamp. A halo of light shines around the bedroom door. The room becomes a landscape of shapes; soft toys become mountains, piles of clothes look like sleeping lions and action figures become silhouettes. As their eyes adjust to the darkness, the children notice a small figure standing amongst the clutter. 'What doll is that?' asks the boy. 'It's one of your figures,' whispers the girl. The stiff little doll just stands there. The children get goosebumps. They know that is not a toy. Suddenly, it runs at them, a mess of long wiry hair and sharp fangs. It's hungry for blood! As the children scream, the cat pounces through the door, grabs the small hungry doll and chews it up. Choking and retching, she vomits up a pile of brown goo and hair ... the remains of the Jenglot!

Jenglots, Indonesian mythical beings, are believed to be living mummies. These brown, long-haired, 15-centimetre shrivelled doll-men are kept as pets and fed on a diet of blood. The people of Java and Sumatra keep specimens of Jenglots in display cases. Amazingly, these monsters have only existed since 1997. Taxidermists, who stuff dead animals to preserve them, have admitted to making hoax versions of the disturbing dolls from monkeys, fish and human hair. But people really do believe they exist, hiding in dark places.

So, next time you see a cat coughing up a hair ball, you may want to thank them for saving you from a Jenglot!

JIANGSHI

CHINA

There are some monster stories where the facts are much worse than the fiction! Like this one ...

When someone died in fifteenth-century China, during the Qing Dynasty, tradition stated that their body must be returned home or it couldn't rest in peace. Transporting a body by cart was expensive if the family were far away. It was cheaper to hire a Taoist monk to 'hop' the body home. Yes, hop it home. The monk may have had several bodies to move, so he hired men who attached the bodies upright to bamboo poles, so they looked alive as they hopped along! It would be bad luck to see this dreadful procession in the dead of night. It looked even worse when the men placed the body on their shoulders, covering it with a black sheet and popping a mask on its face! Out of this terrifying tradition came the Jiangshi: hopping vampires.

Jiangshi, meaning 'stiff bodies', are traditionally dressed in the official costume of the Qing Dynasty. Their flesh is a whitish green and freckled with fungus. By day they rest in graveyards, while at night they start hopping about, looking for victims. ***Hop hop hop***, they move in long lines with arms stiffly outstretched. Stuck to their forehead is a spell – written on paper in chicken's blood – that's used to control them. Jiangshi can be used as deadly weapons, but instead of sucking blood, like usual vampires, Jiangshi feed on qi – life force.

How do you avoid becoming a Jiangshi? Don't let them bite you or let your dead body be reanimated by spells. Be buried properly, never let a cat walk over your coffin and make sure your 'huns' outnumber your 'pos'. Pos are evil and huns are good, and in Chinese folklore everyone has them, but some have more pos than others!

So, how do you survive a Jiangshi attack? You'll need sticky rice to throw, a broom, vinegar, mirrors, black donkeys' hooves, beans and blood from a black dog. Hop to it!

勅令大将軍到此

BLEMMYE

NORTH AFRICA

Good evening ladies and gentlemen, welcome to a special edition of the World's Greatest and Worst Monster Quiz! Tonight, if you answer these questions correctly, you will win ... a car, a games console, a holiday, a cuddly toy or none of these things! Let's get quizzing!

QUESTION ONE

What is a Blemmye?

A. An ape

B. A person hunched down with their head tucked in

C. Someone carrying a shield low down with a face on it

D. A person who can raise their shoulders really high so their heads look low

E. A monster with no head, but its eyes and mouth are on its chest and stomach.

The answer is ... all of them!

QUESTION TWO

Where do Blemmyes come from?

A. Himalayan mountains

B. Nile Delta

C. Africa

D. South America

E. Asia.

The answer is ... all of them!

QUESTION THREE

Where do stories and drawings of Blemmyes appear?

A. On medieval maps

B. In the writings of the Roman author Pliny the Elder

C. In plays by William Shakespeare

D. In old illustrations and woodcuts

E. In voyage accounts by explorers.

The answer is ... all of them!

Congratulations! You have won nothing, but you have learnt that Blemmyes are monsters who suffer at the hands of people's poor eyesight! Since they were first reported in the seventh century, accounts of these creatures have changed. Blemmyes were originally thought to have been a tribe of real people, but over time they became this made-up headless form. They were even drawn in medieval manuscripts and illustrated on maps up to the seventeenth century. But the descriptions of these monsters suffered from human interpretations. Accuracy faded to the point where they are now shown as monsters eating ice creams by the seaside! Who knows the truth behind these creatures, if they were apes mistaken for warriors, or people hiding behind raised shields with scary faces on them? Blemmyes are incredible, have you ever tried eating cold ice cream through your belly button?! Eeek.

ROC

MADAGASCAR AND PERSIA

A feather the length of fifteen strides! Take fifteen big steps and you can imagine the massive size of the Roc, a mythical bird of prey. This huge, soaring bird originated in Arabian fairy tales and sailors' folktales. Rocs can be found crowding the skies in Tolkien's *The Lord of the Rings*, in the voyages of 'Sinbad the Sailor' from *The Arabian Nights* and many other fantasy classics. Marco Polo, a thirteenth-century Italian explorer, described how the Roc could carry elephants in its talons. It would fly over mountains and drop the elephants, smashing them into pieces, so it could eat them. Crows do the same with snails, to crack their shells and eat the soft innards.

Rocs were said to nest on Madagascar, an island in the Indian Ocean, and so-called proof of their existence – a single feather – was brought back from an expedition. But it was probably just a frond from a raffia palm, a tropical tree, which does look feathery.

Other mythological stories place the Roc in Chinese waters, where it lay its eggs along the coastline. If the eggs were destroyed by people, then the Roc would cause tremendous storms and devastation in its fury!

After the eighteenth century, scientists began to untangle the myths and origins of these monster birds. Flying eagles were known to carry lambs in their claws, perhaps this inspired the idea of Rocs carrying elephants? Then the fossil of a Malagasy crowned eagle, the top predator in Madagascar until 1,000 years ago, was discovered. This bird would have eaten lemurs and monkeys, but it was actually the giant and extinct elephant bird who was thought to feast on pygmy hippos. Palaeontologists, scientists who study fossils, also linked the myth to bones of the flightless elephant bird.

Exaggeration, making something seem better or worse than it actually is, and the discovery of new creatures, has fuelled many monster myths. Imagine first seeing an ostrich in a faraway land, and then describing it to people when you returned home. That ostrich would have easily doubled in size in your retelling. Exaggeration is a monster's best friend.

NINKI-NANKA

THE GAMBIA

You are a cryptozoologist – crypto means 'hidden' and zoologists study animals. You are an expert in the study of hidden animals! For this job, you need a healthy belief in the unbelievable, a nose for solving mysteries and a backpack. You are going on an expedition to The Gambia in West Africa!

Pushing through dense jungle and wading through mangrove swamps, the idea of a mythical monster is far from your mind. It's the real monsters that worry you! Crocodiles, cobras, green mambas and monitor lizards ... and that is only the chunkier wildlife! There are so many insects and birds that the air is filled with song and buzz. But forget the known creatures, you are on the hunt for a giant, crested and horned beast, that's dragon-like and crocodile-like, with a 9-metre long giraffe's neck. It's the feared Ninki-Nanka!

The myth goes so far back in time that the Gambian people cannot remember when it began. A local man reported that a pumping station had its pipes ripped to shreds, and the whispered name to blame was the Ninki-Nanka. This caused the workers to panic and hold up mirrors and phones, as the beast cannot stand its own reflection.

In 2006, fellow cryptozoologists went on a Ninki-Nanka expedition. They were thoroughly scientific, interviewing people and studying physical evidence, including a monster scale. They had a map where an X marked the burial site of a monstrous carcass that had washed up on Bungalow Beach in the 1980s. A treasure map for a monster! Sadly, the tide had washed away the carcass, and the scale was plastic, but the team did reach some conclusions. They believe the Ninki-Nanka could be one of three things: a monitor lizard, which grew to 3 metres long, a mythical giant snake called the crowing crested cobra or the washed-up carcass of a small whale or dolphin.

But you are a cryptozoologist. You'll leave no stone unturned: there's no jungle too deep or sighting too unbelievable. Keep looking!

OTHER NAMES Jerff, Vielfras

GERMANY AND SWEDEN

It's your birthday, and you've eaten lunch, followed by cake, more cake and a tiny bit more cake. You then have dinner, followed by another slice of cake because, after all, it is your birthday. But now you feel totally stuffed, bloated like an overfilled balloon. Why did you eat so much?!

If you were the Gulon, you would feel like this every day. This monster eats, eats and eats, until its body is as tight as a drum, and its legs are hardly able to carry its stomach, which is crammed full of animal carcasses and rotting meat. The Gulon eats animals twice its own size until it is fit to burst. In fact, the name of this Scandinavian legend – Gulon – is very close to the ancient language Latin word gulo, meaning glutton or greed. Before its tummy expands, it is about the size of a large dog, with cat-like features and shaggy brown fur. It's often mistaken for a wolverine, a ferocious meat-eater that hunts at night and eats whatever they can find. But the similarities don't stop there. In Latin, wolverines are called 'gulo gulo', again meaning glutton!

Wolverines, though, can only dream of what the Gulon has in store for us. A brilliant, but totally disgusting, signature move. It finds two trees close together, walks up to the tree trunks and forces its way through the gap, like a tube of furry toothpaste being squeezed. Pushing itself through this space takes immense effort and achieves something horrible. The Gulon forces out its own body weight of POO! It has been poo-mangled! The poo is now piled in a stinky dirty mound and its guts are empty. It's ready to start eating again. What a relief. Anyone have an air freshener?!

Gluttony is viewed as a bad habit in many cultures. Stories and monster legends show it as unhealthy and antisocial behaviour. The Gulon is a dirty monster, unsatisfied and greedy, mostly found squashed between two trees, surrounded by mountains of steaming poo.

Is it enough to put you off that cake?

MEDUSA

OTHER NAMES Gorgo

GREECE

Hissssssssss, rattle, rattle, hisssssssssssssss. Echoing in the darkness, all Perseus can hear is the sound of hissing and the rhythmic clicking of rattlesnake tails. The sounds fill the low chamber and flickering torches cast hideous shadows. He cautiously holds up his shining bronze shield to look behind him. The warped reflection shows there's nothing there. He moves softly between pillars, hunting the creature that he must never directly look at. The hissing is getting nearer, the creature is also searching for him.

The shield still doesn't show her, but Perseus must not be tempted to look. All around him are stone statues of people who came but never left. Once they were flesh and blood, but one look from her and they turned to stone.

Hissssssss. She is here! Her shadow ripples on the ceiling, showing coiled shapes above a woman's body. She moves towards Perseus' hiding place, and he grips the sword given to him by the gods. He looks again in the bronze shield ... Oh the horror! The reflection shows a twisted and menacing gorgon. Where once her long hair would have flowed, there are hundreds of writhing serpents, their fangs oozing venom. Her eyes burn orange with hatred. She sees Perseus, and her shriek makes the snakes go into a frenzy as she charges at his reflection. In one swipe, Perseus cuts off her snake-heavy head, which falls to the floor oozing acidic blood. Still he must not look at Medusa, as even in death her stare kills!

In ancient Greek mythology, Medusa was one of three gorgon sisters living on the island of Sarpedon. She was once beautiful, but a curse transformed her into a monster. After killing her, Perseus flew away on the winged horse Pegasus, with her head in a sack. Blood from the sack dripped onto the Sahara desert making vipers, and leaked into the Red Sea creating coral reefs. It also created the double-headed serpent Amphisbaena. Medusa is truly a magnificent ancient monster.

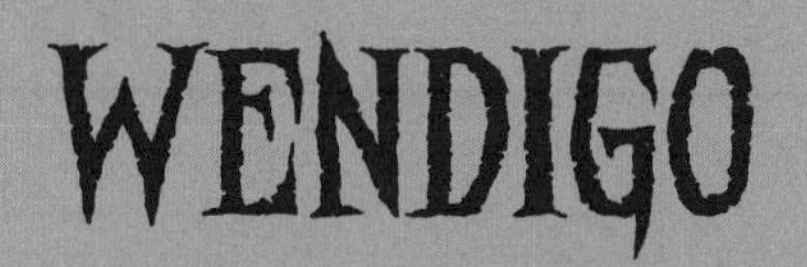

WENDIGO

OTHER NAMES Wetiko

CANADA AND USA

'HELLO!' you shout across the lake. 'Hello, hello, hello,' eerily echoes back over the water. As the sun sets, you are standing alone by Lake Windigo on Star Island, in Minnesota, USA. Incredibly, this lake is surrounded by another lake. How? Star Island sits on Lake Cass, where only canoes are allowed on the crystal water. Suddenly, the air chills ...

'Hello!' your voice returns again. But this time you didn't shout ... 'Hello!' it gurgles.

You whip around. Behind you there is something standing, half hidden in the tree line.

Oh no, you see the pale skeletal thing step out from the behind the trees followed by a smell! A vile, sharp smell. It looks angry, with eyes sunken in bone sockets. It must be 5 metres tall at least. It is hissing, trying to mimic your voice again, as it walks towards you leaving bloody footprints. 'HELLO!' its voice shrieks and rasps. This is the thing the Algonquian Native American people call Wendigo! The cannibal monster is the 'spirit of lonely places', and it's constantly hungry for flesh.

There are many variations of the Wendigo told in different tribal stories across the USA and Canada. Its name may vary, but everyone agrees on its violent and evil behaviour. It is a monster that represents fears of hunger and cold and warns against greed and destroying environments.

The Wendigo appears in film and fiction and is a fantastically vile character that lurks in the woods, eating or possessing people. But there have also been hundreds of sightings of it from the 1800s up to the present day, mostly from near the Cave of the Wendigo, in Kenora, Ontario, USA. As recently as 2019, the story of an unknown creature screaming and howling in the woods in Minnesota, USA reached the global news. Nobody could identify the sounds recorded by a hunter and his family, but they seemed unnatural! The question was asked, was it Wendigo screaming? They had the good sense to run before they found out.

WELCOME
TO
LAKE
WINDIGO

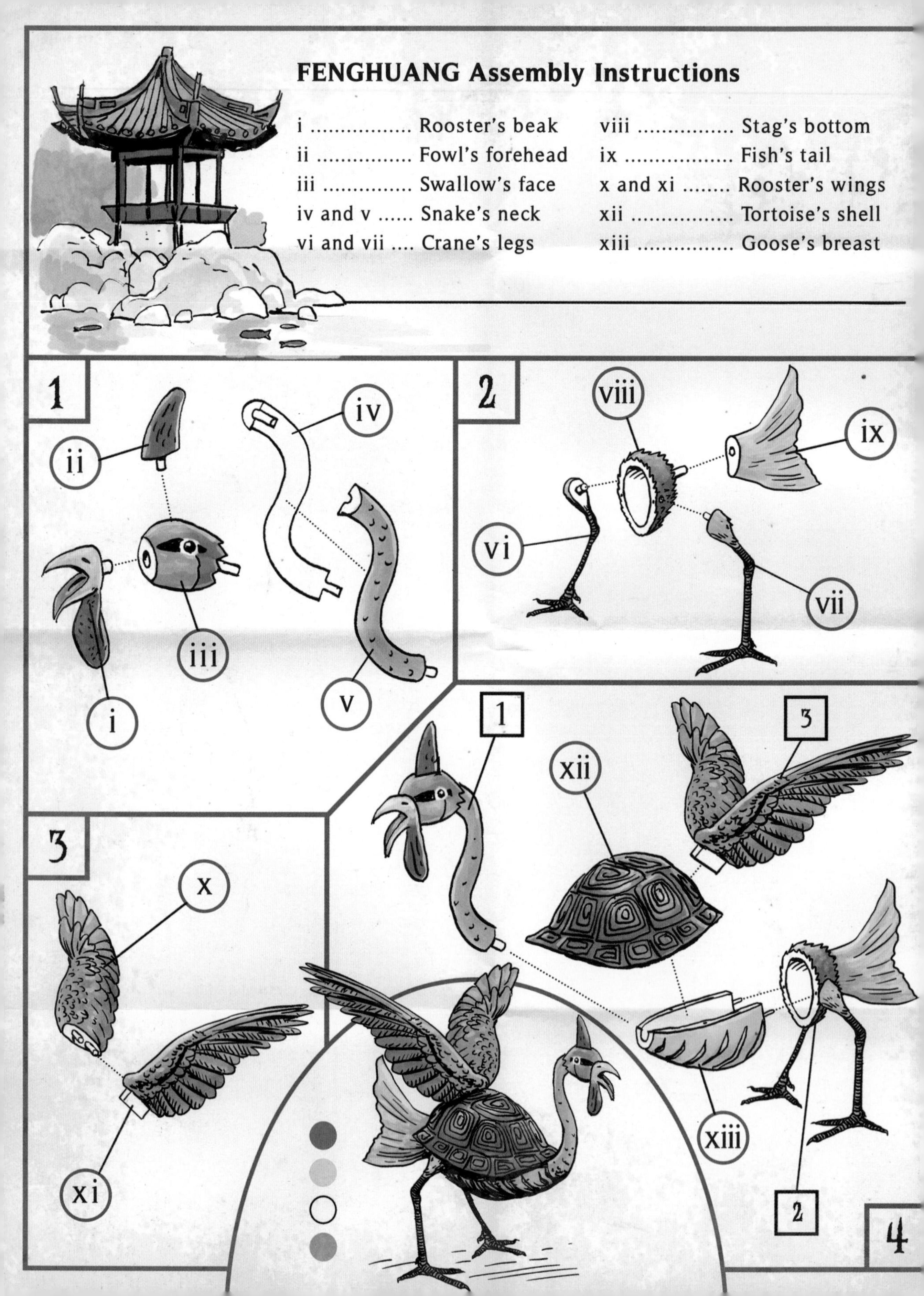
FENGHUANG Assembly Instructions
i .... Rooster's beak
ii .... Fowl's forehead
iii .... Swallow's face
iv and v ...... Snake's neck
vi and vii .... Crane's legs
viii .... Stag's bottom
ix .... Fish's tail
x and xi .... Rooster's wings
xii .... Tortoise's shell
xiii .... Goose's breast
1
ii
iv
i
iii
v
2
viii
ix
vi
vii
3
x
xi
1
3
xii
xiii
2
4

FENGHUANG

OTHER NAMES Chinese Phoenix, Hou-Ou

CHINA

Do you love making models? How about one of a traditional Chinese bird that is sometimes called the Chinese Phoenix and is over 8,000 years old? Grab some glue and feel a sense of peace as you make the Fenghuang.

Let's start with attaching the tortoise to the moon; right where is the moon? The fish attaches to the planets, then the rooster to the swallow and fowl to the sky, erm, wait, no let's start again. You might need to unglue some bits ...

The bird's beak comes from a rooster, and the face from a swallow. It has a fowl's forehead, snake's neck, goose's breast, rooster's wings, tortoise's shell, stag's bottom, crane's legs and fish's tail. Glue it all together! Surely that can't be right, this is a bird, not a fish or mammal or serpent! The different parts of this confusing creature – the Fenghuang – represent important elements; the head is the sky, eyes are the sun, back is the moon, wings are the wind, feet are the earth and tail is the planets.

Time to paint. But choose the colours carefully as they have special meanings to Chinese people. Black, white, red, yellow and green are sacred colours. The ancient philosopher Confucius, who was born in 551 BCE, placed special values on these colours. Black is the colour of heaven and water, white means death and purity, red is for happiness and fire, yellow is for heroism and freedom and green is used for health and harmony.

In Chinese mythology, Fenghuang rules over all other birds and features on sculptures, ceramics, jade jewellery and in paintings. It is made up of the male and female birds Feng and Huang and only appears in places of peace and spiritual balance. Not to be mistaken as just a pretty decoration, it is often shown catching large serpents in its huge talons.

The sightings of Fenghuang are a symbol of change in Chinese royalty. This beautiful 3-metre-tall bird also has the voice of joy, laughter and beauty!

Really hope your model can do justice to this epic bird!

BOGEYMAN

OTHER NAMES Bogge, Boogieman

WORLDWIDE

'Goodnight, sleep tight, don't let the Bogeyman bite!'

Alone, in bed, in a moonlit room, there's just you and the threat of the Bogeyman. Your cupboard door is ajar, and it makes you uneasy. Lying down, you wonder what is under your bed. The duvet hangs off one side, perhaps something is pulling it? Is something lying under there, waiting for you to fall asleep? Maybe a hairy hand, just visible, or a hooded thing, breathing heavily. STOP! You switch on the lamp, close the cupboard and look under the bed. All is fine, just the usual clutter.

Once again in the dark, you stare at the moon framed in the open window. You get up to look at the moonlit garden and the field beyond. The shadows are long, and the cornfield behind the house is making a gentle whispering noise. There is a scarecrow, which is funny as it wasn't there earlier when you played in the garden. Its sackcloth head is cocked to one side with a tall hat sitting on it, and the body is stiffly rocking in the breeze. The corn sways, the scarecrow turns and the hairs on your arms prickle. Scarecrows are for scaring birds, not people. Back in bed you imagine your mum's voice again, 'don't let the Bogeyman bite'.

The Bogeyman scares children, and adults, worldwide and takes many different forms depending on the country, culture and even household. Everyone has their own Bogeyman, which represents people's fears. Since the 1500s, the Bogeyman has been used to get children to sleep, stay safe and fear strangers. It comes from the Old English word 'bogge', meaning something frightening, hobgoblin or evil.

Now, just have one last look out of your window. No! The scarecrow pole is empty, a trail of flattened corn leads to the garden gate. A rustling makes you turn to look at your bedroom door where a straw hand is pushing it open ...

LESHY

OTHER NAMES Lord of the Forest

RUSSIA

Thick fog hovers over the damp, mossy ground and swirls around the black tree trunks in the middle of the Russian forest. Above, the stars glimmer over the tree canopy, while down on the ground everything is dark, but alive! Mushrooms grow in a circle around the trees as a world of miniature life scuttles on the woodland floor. The sounds of the forest are trees brushing and bending, screeching owls, howling wolves and bears grunting nearby. Snakes disturb the leaves, which swirl and curl up to form a pillar of twigs, leaves and dirt, and within the moving whirlwind the form of a massive man emerges! He is twice human height. Branches grow from his arched back as if he was a living tree, bone horns sprout from his brow and he has sharp claws. His eyes burn bright and dangerous. Those howls and grunts grow louder as his packs of animals circle him. All around are wolves and bears that he protects.

Leshy, Lord of the Forest, is more forest than man. He has immense strength, can shapeshift into animals and people and use your voice to mimic and bewitch you. He sometimes lures travellers deep into his woods to their death and takes children who are unloved, passing them to the forest to bring up.

Leshy has a wife, Kikimora of the Swamp, who is half-human, half-insect and leaves wet footprints when she enters houses. Once inside, she steals the breath of sleeping residents! Leshy and Kikimora also have children, leshonkis, who live wild in the forest with them.

There is no way of knowing how far back the Leshy myth goes, as Slavic stories are passed on by word-of-mouth, and there is only written evidence from the sixth century onwards. Many Russian people used to firmly believe that Leshy was real. In a human disguise, he loves to gamble, and there is suspicion that he gambled away all the squirrels in Russia in a bet.

EUROPEAN DRAGON

EUROPE

Clang! Clang! Clang! The village bell tower sounds out the alarm, warning the villagers to run, hide or jump into the river! Screaming people flee in every direction, toppling carts and startling horses, who break free and gallop out of the doomed town.

In the eerie quiet that follows, an orange sunset contains no birdsong or human sounds. There's only a distant black shape and a rhythmic beating as a creature flies closer and closer to the village. As it descends from up high, the sun's last rays illuminate scales, horns, leathery wings and extended claws. With an open mouth and smoking nostrils, it fires a plume of orange flames from its huge and powerful mouth. The jet of fire pours over the town's straw rooftops, and as those leathery wings beat, they fan the fire that burns the village to charcoal and dust. Only a few stone buildings survive, like broken teeth amongst the cinders.

Dragons! Deadly, mythical creatures from storytelling, religious texts, Greek writing, Roman mythology and modern films, TV and books, whose popularity is as strong as ever. The European Dragon is an ancient creature coiled within a treasure-filled lair. Once thought to be serpent-like, some describe it as a silver-mouthed, silk-bodied worm like a windsock. Pliny the Elder, a Roman writer, tells of Dragon, the elephant-eating snake monster. Ladon, a 100-headed dragon, was slain by Heracles in Greek stories, and the Greek Hydra was another famed dragonish beast.

Between the eleventh and thirteenth centuries, dragon mania was at its peak. If they had television then, most programmes would have been dragon-filled! The snakes from earlier tales became more lizardy over time, with bat-like wings and venomous bites. Heroes and saints have always successfully slain these monsters and earned their place in legends. Dragons remind us of dinosaurs, from the age when creatures were terrible and huge, but they enrich so many books and films that they may be the most popular monster of them all!

YULE CAT

OTHER NAMES Jólakötturinn

ICELAND

It is Christmas Eve, or *Aðfangadagur* in Icelandic, and the snow is falling softly onto the already deep snowdrifts outside the window. Inside, the house is bejewelled with Christmas decorations. A brother and sister are full of excitement because, as part of Icelandic Christmas tradition, they can open their presents tonight.

The mystery of those wrapped bundles under the spruce tree will soon be revealed! After a delicious meal of smoked lamb, corn, cabbage and a sugared leaf bread, the children open their gifts! 'A jumper!', 'A computer game!' and so on, until all the presents lay opened.

The brother stares at his sister's gifts. 'What?' she demands, 'Where are the clothes?' he whispers. 'Clothes are boring,' she replies. The boy puts on his new jumper and goes to the window, looking past the falling snow, towards the horizon. He searches for a monster ...

In a cave nearby, Grýla the giantess, her husband Leppalúði, their thirteen prankster sons – the 'Yule Lads' – and their hungry pet, the massive Yule Cat, are all leaving for town. They will steal badly behaved children, put potatoes in the shoes of the slightly naughty ones and the cat will eat any child that did not receive clothes for Christmas! Yes, you are cat food if you do not have a scarf, socks or jumper on your Christmas list.

Meowwwwwwwwwwwwwww! The Yule Cat pads over the houses as if they are toys, staring in windows at the knitwear on the children. ***Hiss!*** She keeps prowling, her dark and angry eyes narrow as her furry belly rumbles. All the children have new clothes! The last house she peeks into is the sleeping brother and sister's home. The boy is wearing his jumper. Ah ha! She has no new clothes! Dinner is served. As the Yule Cat's paw reaches her, the cover falls away showing her new socks! ***Meeeewwwww, hisssssss!*** The cat disappears into the night, and the brother smiles in his sleep, knowing the gift of one of his presents to his sleeping sister saved her from the Yule Cat!

TIGRE CAPIANGO

OTHER NAMES Runa Uturuncu, Were-Jaguar, Yaguareté-Avá

SOUTH AMERICA

'General Quiroga, sir, they are all gone!' The Argentine General nodded. The young messenger enquired, 'But why have the enemy run away?' General Facundo Quiroga simply answered, 'Tigre Capiangos.'

General Quiroga's soldiers were all Were-Jaguars! What general would not wish for a battalion of soldiers with the power to shapeshift into ferocious wild cats? Who could stand and face a wall of half-human, half-jaguar beings, with the strength and agility of the jaguar combined with the obedience and strategy of the soldier? Imagine that army! Facing a human war must be devastating and dangerous, but to battle supernatural monsters is another level of terror. During the Argentine Civil War in the 1800s, accounts of General Quiroga's incredible battalion became part of legend.

Were-Jaguars, Were-Tigers, Were-Cats – think werewolves but cat-like! – are found in many cultures and have been chiselled in stone and painted in caves. They span the South American continent from Argentina's Tigre Capiangos, the Runa Uturuncus of the Andes mountains and the Yaguareté-Avá of the Guarani culture, who mostly live in Paraguay.

But are these creatures just humans wearing the skins of big cats for ceremony, or is it to show they should be feared? The idea of transforming into an animal is an important part of ceremonies in Aztec culture in South America. The jaguar warriors were the best of Aztec military might! They would dress in a jaguar's skin and feel their power and wild strength overtake them. The skin covered their whole body, with just their painted face showing inside the open jaws of the dead animal. They trained to kill their enemy and prove their place as ultimate predators.

On the Serrezuela mountains in Spain, carvings were discovered that showed human footprints that seem to change into cat pawprints, going back thousands of years. The prints seem to show a wild dance pattern where the dancer started off human and gradually became a cat. Who knows how long humans have been changing into cats! Or is it the other way around?

KRAKEN

ICELAND, NORWAY AND SWEDEN

The telegraph machine frantically begins to tap out a message in a series of short dots and long dashes that's being sent by a boat out at sea. On the mainland, the Norwegian telegraph operator quickly translates the code into words, terrifying words ...

Tentakler, øyet, boblebad, brøl, tentakler som klemmer, skipet er splintret, vi drukner.

Looking pale and worried, he reads it aloud: 'Tentacles, the eye, whirlpool, roar, tentacles squeezing, the ship is splintered, we drown.'

The slip of paper describes a ship's last moments out on the Norwegian Sea, between Iceland and Norway. Then the machine taps out a final word ... KRAKEN!

It's the mighty sea monster of Norse sagas, sightings and superstition! The Kraken is a gigantic cephalopod, a type of colossal squid or giant octopus that's so large it can snap a ship in two and create monstrous whirlpools. It rises from the freezing ocean depths, flailing its 15-metre-long barbed tentacles, and its huge, globulous eyes – the size of dinner plates – stare at the destruction it causes. It crushes ships, sucking in everything in its path: the wreckage, the crew, the very sea it swims in!

The Kraken has been reported by so many seafarers that it was included in sixteenth-century nature books. It was described as a giant octopus that could be mistaken for an island out at sea.

But can it really exist? Well, the giant Pacific octopus can grow to 18 metres long and weigh up to a tonne – as heavy as a great white shark. And a colossal squid captured in 2007 was 10 metres long! These creatures are wonders of the sea. They have the biggest eyes in the animal kingdom, blue blood, three hearts and hooks on their suckers. Perhaps the disturbances in the waters were undersea volcanoes causing waves, whirlpools and lands to rise up. But the sea is vast and there is plenty of room to grow, so maybe, just maybe, the Kraken is down there ...

MERLION

SINGAPORE

As the dive boat sails out of Singapore's harbour, the tourists on board snap photos of the ferocious white sculpture that shoots water from its jaws. The Merlion stands 9 metres high against a backdrop of shining glass skyscrapers and is the mighty symbol of Singapore. As the statue disappears from view, the tourists pull on their scuba gear. They will dive in the waters around Singapore, excited by the promise of seeing marine turtles, parrot fish and black-tipped sharks.

The sunshine reaches the depths of the turquoise sea, where swaying sea fans dance in the currents. ***Splash!*** The divers drop overboard. Through the small porthole of the scuba masks, they wave at each other, swimming through the air bubbles from their oxygen tanks. The exquisite reef is covered with clownfish and angel fish, swimming through the underwater plants that flow like hair. ***Click, click, click***, the divers snap photos. Then the reef floor shudders and lifts, a monstrous fish rises with the head of a lion and a mouth full of fangs, sucking in the sea water and small fish. The sea vibrates with a sound, which above water would be a deafening roar. ***Snap, snap, snap***, the camera clicks as it falls to the ocean floor. Bubbles erupt from the divers' mouths as they scream. The Merlion is all around them, tangling them in his mane.

The Merlion sounds like a classic beast from the deep, but it's a human-made monster. In 1964, Alec Fraser-Brunner designed the Merlion as the mascot for Singapore. The lion head indicates the city's strength, and the fish tail represents Singapore's fishing heritage. The huge, 70-tonne statue was sculpted by Lim Nang Seng and placed at the head of the harbour. There have never been lions in Singapore, but the city's name translates as Lion City thanks to a mythological lion sighting when the area was discovered. The lion asked for the city to be called Lion City, and so it was. Who could argue with a mythical talking lion?

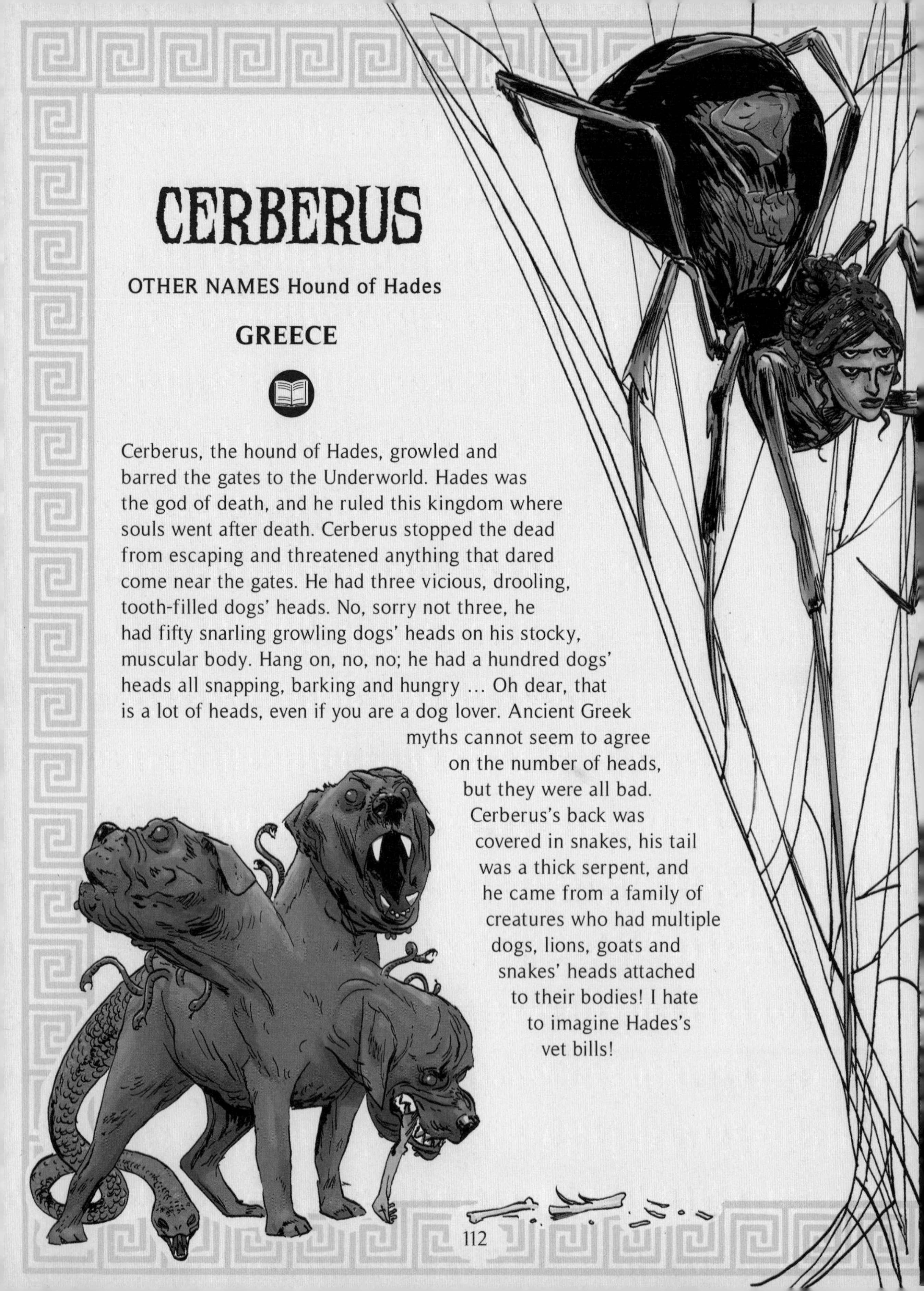

CERBERUS

OTHER NAMES Hound of Hades

GREECE

Cerberus, the hound of Hades, growled and barred the gates to the Underworld. Hades was the god of death, and he ruled this kingdom where souls went after death. Cerberus stopped the dead from escaping and threatened anything that dared come near the gates. He had three vicious, drooling, tooth-filled dogs' heads. No, sorry not three, he had fifty snarling growling dogs' heads on his stocky, muscular body. Hang on, no, no; he had a hundred dogs' heads all snapping, barking and hungry … Oh dear, that is a lot of heads, even if you are a dog lover. Ancient Greek myths cannot seem to agree on the number of heads, but they were all bad. Cerberus's back was covered in snakes, his tail was a thick serpent, and he came from a family of creatures who had multiple dogs, lions, goats and snakes' heads attached to their bodies! I hate to imagine Hades's vet bills!

ARACHNE

GREECE

Beautiful, talented and proud Arachne was a mortal; a normal human with an extraordinary talent for spinning cloth. Her cloth was so delicate, artistic and skilled that people travelled to marvel at her creations. Arachne was boastful, and she saw her talent as being almost god-like. From above, the Greek goddess Athena was listening. Athena was a wonderful spinner, and the Greek myth tells of her setting a challenge to Arachne, a spin-off. Both created incredible cloth, but Arachne's was finer and depicted a scene mocking the gods! Athena, quietly seething said, 'Well done, Arachne, you must spin forever because you are so good!' And cruelly, she cursed Arachne and transformed her into a gigantic spiderwoman, with eight long black legs, forced to spin webs for eternity! Her cursed female face was perched on her bulbous abdomen. She would crawl and spin webs across the ceilings of the temples. Gods are very poor losers!

AMPHISBAENA

OTHER NAMES Amphivena, Mother of Ants

GREECE

In Greek mythology, Perseus fought and killed the evil gorgon Medusa and triumphantly flew off on the winged horse Pegasus. Medusa's severed, snake-haired head was held in a sack, oozing blood. The moment a drop of her acidic blood dripped onto the desert sands below, something began to grow. Boiling and frothing, suddenly a huge plume of scales and skin erupted from the desert floor. Thrashing and biting, the giant body of Amphisbaena emerged with a snake head hissing at either end of its huge body. Amphisbaena fed mainly on dead bodies as it slithered across the desert. It was also named Mother of Ants, as it was thought to eat so many. Later stories of the beast claim it had wings, with lizard-like legs and looked similar to a dragon. Amphisbaena was an impressive monster; its only issue was how to go to the toilet with a head at both ends?

MOKELE-MBEMBE

CONGO RIVER BASIN

Could dinosaurs still live on Earth today? One answer comes from science and looks at the theory of evolution, the other is based on myth and mystery!

Coelacanth fish have existed on Earth for 360 million years! They were thought to be extinct for 65 million years, along with dinosaurs, and only remained as fossils. That was until this 2-metre-long heavily scaled creature was found alive and well in 1938 off the coast of South Africa! If this fish can hide from our inquisitive eyes for millions of years, then perhaps a much larger prehistoric creature could be laying low somewhere.

Since 1909, hunters, travellers and expedition groups have told stories about an incredible beast living in the rainforest of the Congo River Basin in central Africa. Described as half-elephant, half-dragon, it eats hippopotamus and attacks canoes. It has a long, scaled tail like an alligator, brownish skin and a long neck with a single tooth or horn. Reports of this monster, known as Mokele-Mbembe, were shared worldwide from 1909 up until 2012, when film crews searched for it. This animal would probably, if drawn by a police sketch artist, look very much like an apatosaurus dinosaur or brontosaurus! But surely a dinosaur cannot survive until now, can it?

Palaeontologists, zoologists, geneticists, biologists – all the 'ists'! – will explain that dinosaurs cannot exist today due to natural selection and extinction. So how can we explain over 100 years of reports of the Mokele-Mbembe? In 2001, a tribe of people living in the Congo River Basin who believed in the monster were shown animal illustrations to see if they could point out the Mokele-Mbembe. 'That's it!' they said and pointed to a picture of a rhinoceros! Rhinos are incredibly rare, if ever seen in the Congo River Basin, but perhaps a shared memory of these dangerous creatures has been passed down? The imprint of the monster is not just hiding in the dense jungle, but also deep within the tribe's memory!

CYCLOPS

GREECE

Run and hide! Here comes the giant hulking monster of Greek mythology, the son of Poseidon! His huge bulging eye wildly searches for his next meal as he crushes stones under his feet and steps over small mountains. This uncivilised shepherd can barely care for his cattle because of his lust for people-eating. Aaagh, it's Cyclops!

No, that's not a description of Cyclops. Let's start again ...

Son of Uranus and goddess Gaea, the hard-working giant blacksmith tirelessly served the god Hephaestus in the belly of the active volcano Mount Etna, near Sicily. An expert craftsman, his one giant orb of an eye was so skilled at creating items of perfection that he forged the Greek god Zeus's thunderbolt!

Stop! That is not Cyclops! He wasn't a blacksmith. Try again ...

Cyclops was an ancient builder of temples and palaces, such as Mycenae and the hillfort Tiryns in Greece. His immensely strong arms carried stones larger than any man could shift, and he built the walls so expertly that they still stand today! Why, the Greeks even named his brick-laying style after him: cyclopean, laid like our house bricks are today. He is no one-eyed people-eating monster, but he does like to swallow goats and sheep, whole!

For 2,720 years, stories of the Cyclops have been told and retold, placing him as either a major villain or a skilled servant to the gods. The only things the differing tales agree on are his looks! The ancient Greeks believed that Cyclops existed, but some say the one-eyed myth came from the single eye patches that blacksmiths wore. Others connect it to the discovery of prehistoric dwarf elephant bones. Their skulls had large central holes for breathing that looked like an eye socket!

Cyclops' image is mainly that of the dumb, angry giant who crushes anyone who sees him, but behind that huge eye is a brain full of exquisite skill and care.

BABA YAGA

OTHER NAMES The Witch of the East

RUSSIA

If you go into the Russian forests, deep enough to enter the world of folklore and fairy tales, beware! Beware Baba Yaga. For hundreds of years this scary old witch has stalked the ancient Russian woodlands looking for lost children. Come into the dark forest and meet her ...

A wooden hut without windows or a door is a strange sight nestled in this creepy forest. But not as strange as the chicken legs that hold up the hut, the fact that it turns like a spinning top or that the fence is made from human leg bones. Open the bony gate and breathe in the delicious cooking smell coming from the smoking chimney. 'Hello?' you call, walking around the hut. 'Anyone home?' The hut lowers onto the dirt, and a door appears and opens; you hold your breath. The homeowner's face is covered in warts and creased like an old dish cloth, her few teeth are black, and green spit wets her smiling lips. This is Baba Yaga.

The hag's clothes are ragged and stained, covering a thin body. Her smell is eye-watering boggy and eggy. She holds a pestle, a rounded tool for grinding seeds and bones, and her mortar, a heavy bowl, is behind her on the table. Through the open door, you see something bubbling on the stove and roasting in the giant oven. 'Coming for tea?' she asks. What do you think? Are you hungry? Because Baba Yaga is, and it will be your leg bone in her fence and your skull on her gate!

The Russian folktale of Baba Yaga was used to scare children and stop them from straying into forests and talking to strangers. The Witch of the East, as the Russians call her, has been the complex villain in many stories. Although, Baba Yaga does have a caring side, and if you do not displease her, she will let you go. Otherwise you will see the inside of her immense oven, and be the leftovers stuck in her blackened teeth!

THETIS LAKE MONSTER

CANADA

The day was hot, the year was 1972 and the place was Victoria, in Canada's British Columbia. Two boys were enjoying a day fishing on Thetis Lake. The beautiful lake attracted locals to fish and swim in the cool water. But in the depths, something stirred, churning up the lakebed with huge webbed hands. On the fishing platform the boys were laughing and kicking the water with bare feet, unaware of the danger below.

Up it swam! Scarily fast, like a shark sensing blood, rushing towards the surface where the boys' feet dangled. The monster's eyes widened with hunger. The boys caught a flash of the monster's burning-red eyes, like two underwater flares.

What is that?! Then a pointed head emerged on a neck sliced with gills ... that's no fish! It lunged, a clawed hand broke through the surface with a wet roar ... ***Aagghhhhhhh.*** The boys' screams echoed across the lake, where two other boys saw the attack by the human-sized silver-scaled monster!

The Royal Canadian Mounted Police interviewed the four boys, who described a monster just like the one from the film *Monster from the Surf*, which they had watched the night before. Pointed head, silver gills, webbed clawed hands. Hmmmmm? The police found no actual evidence of the creature on Thetis Lake, other than the boys' stories. But soon there were other reports describing the same gill man from the monster movies.

And so the Thetis Lake Monster lives! Once a story is reported in the papers and investigated, it trickles into urban legend. One day the lake was just a lake, the next it had a monster legend.

The Thetis Lake Monster was a hoax. A deliberate lie to create a false event or story, where the people who tell it are fully aware it is fake. The boys later admitted they lied, there was no monster. But people started to look for it and swear they saw it. People love monsters. Hoaxes fade, but the monsters live on. All a monster needs to survive is curiosity and belief.

WOLPERTINGER

OTHER NAMES Woibbadinga, Wolperdinger

GERMANY

What has happened to you?! Why do you smell so awful, even though you have taken baths and scrubbed yourself? And what is that?! Why do you have thick, matted fur on your hand!? It looks like you have been the victim of Germany's mysterious and confusing Wolpertinger.

You followed a needle-strewn path in the Bavarian forest of south-east Germany, tiptoeing in the moonlight to hide behind a large tree trunk. There, in the clearing, perched on a mound was what appeared to be a rabbit. But it was no ordinary rabbit. This rabbit had wings, antlers, fangs, long pheasant legs and was staring at the moon. The famous mythological Wolpertinger was right there in front of you, and it looked absurd. You edged closer, your foot clumsily cracking a twig, causing it to turn and bare its fangs. Flying at you, it screeched, spraying a stinking liquid in your direction that will take seven years to wash off! Seven years! And then it nipped you. Just one drop of saliva from this bizarre monster caused you to grow thick fur.

Of course, the Wolpertinger is a ridiculous hybrid monster that could not exist in real life. But even though it seems silly, it has been hunted and captured since the 1800s. No pub or hunting lodge would be complete without a stuffed Wolpertinger. Tall tales and hoaxes on tourists have carried this legend through the centuries. Making a creature from bits and pieces of different animals, like a gory jigsaw puzzle, has created thousands of these fake specimens. But why can't they exist? Because species cannot breed to make hybrids like this, no matter how fun they look. Animals can mutate, or change, but this is usually to benefit their lives in some way. They cannot change into another species, or combine five different species as the Wolpertinger has! Biology has rules that control mutations in animals. Monsters just don't care about science. And the duck-billed platypus has some explaining to do!

LOU CARCOLH

OTHER NAMES Carcolhr

FRANCE

'I love snails.' You don't hear that said very often, certainly not by gardeners, and certainly not by the gardeners in the pretty French hillside town of Hastingues. They don't love snails, or snakes. More precisely, they don't love giant serpent snails that have tentacles that stretch for miles and eat people whole! They would rather not be neighbours with them, but they are! For under their feet, beneath their white painted stone houses, lie the caves where Lou Carcolh dwells ...

Though not seen for at least fifty years, this gigantic, slime-oozing, hairy and hungry mollusc-snake has become a firm monster legend in Hastingues, France. Its shell is as high as a church ceiling, and its pulsating, slippery body fills the inside of the cave in the hillside. Its beady eyes extend on long stalks above a gaping mouth. People have entered the caves of the creature and, other than slime trails, they have never been seen again. The Lou Carcolh rarely slides out of its cave nest. It doesn't need to because it uncoils its long, sticky tentacles that are covered in small spikes called radula, just under the dirt. They stretch far from its cave and wait to feel the vibrations of dinner, like a spider sensing a fly on its web, and drags it back to the cave.

Legend tells us of another Lou Carcolh. In the seventeenth century, a merchant bravely stole a clutch of its eggs and sailed to the Americas. But during a storm the eggs rolled overboard and landed in Greenhaven, USA, where Lou Carcolh 2, the Sequel emerged!

Snails are incredible; land snails have lungs, sea snails have gills. The largest sea snail is 1 metre long, weighing 18 kilograms, about the weight of a baboon! The African land snail can measure 38 centimetres and weigh the same as a porcupine! Snails use only two brain cells, one to ask 'Am I hungry?' and the other 'Where's the food?' Just those two simple questions on Lou Carcolh's mind are two questions too many.

FIJI
MERMAID

FIJI MERMAID

OTHER NAMES Cancan Merman, Japanese Mermaid

FIJI, JAPAN AND USA

Roll up, Roll up! Ladies and gentlemen, prepare yourselves, for what you are about to see will mesmerise, delight and appall! From the deepest oceans, where creatures swim and crawl and no human eye has seen, to the furthest reaches of the globe, we present to you a truly special treasure. Preserved and carried from Japan to the USA, in the suitcase of a man who paid a fortune to own it. Travelling across the very seas it lived in and placed here for you to enjoy for just 1 shilling a look ...

Behold the wonder, the majesty of the Fiji Mermaid!

The year was 1842, and eager Victorians shuffled forward into the dim and dramatically draped tent of P.T. Barnum's American Museum Circus. As they pushed their way through the crowds surrounding the glass dome, the audience saw a frightful sight.

If they had expected to see a beautiful mermaid, with glinting scales and a shell bra, they would have been very disappointed. Before them was a dried-up skeleton with the head and body of a monkey, long hair and a fish-like tail curled up beneath it. The strange, ugly specimen looked like a combination of melted chocolate and dead fish!

This was the first 'captured' mermaid after centuries of mythology and sightings. There have been hundreds of specimens of the Fiji Mermaid ever since Captain Eade bought the original in 1822. Each were made from the skeletons of monkeys and fish, or sculpted from papier-mâché.

There is little doubt these oddities were hoaxes made to shock and delight people, but this should not diminish the genuine sightings and belief in mermaids that people have held for centuries. Mermaids have been immortalised throughout history. Sailors have feared them for their Siren songs, which lure ships to the ocean's depths. We have no idea of the undiscovered creatures living in our seas. Why couldn't there be merpeople in the deep blue waters?

TENJŌNAME

JAPAN

'In the cold of winter, tall ceilings swallow the lantern light', or so the Japanese monk Yoshida Kenko wrote in the fourteenth century. Old houses were built with high ceilings to cool homes down during hot Japanese summers. But in winter, the ceilings would freeze over and the oil lamp light couldn't reach that high, creating a space where monsters lurked.

Have you ever noticed a dirty mark on your bedroom ceiling, maybe a water stain, cobwebs or dead moth you have never seen before? A greasy mark where you threw a sticky toy that stuck there for weeks. You stare at it, wondering if it was always there? Never mind, you pull up the duvet, as it's chilly and dark outside. Winter makes your warm bed so cosy.

In the middle of the night you hear something, ***slurp, slurp, scuttle***. Is it rats in the roof? Pipes gurgling? Something drips onto your forehead, but you can't see what because it's so dark. ***Drip, slurrrp, drip, scuttle.*** Too scared to look up again or move, you pull the duvet over your head and try to sleep! In the morning, after a restless night, you wake to winter sunshine. You look up at your ceiling and there, where the marks, cobwebs and moths had been, is a thick slime trail. Urgh! You have been visited by Tenjōname! And you are lucky that you did not look up at him as just one glimpse of his dirty habits would have meant certain death!

Tenjōname means 'ceiling licker', and it is one of Japan's strangest *yokai*, or demons. These monsters lurk at the boundaries between things; outside and inside, sea and land, night and day. They were harmless until their personalities were rewritten in the 1920s to make them more deadly and a little less, er, silly! There is another Tenjō creature, called Tenjō Kudari. Luckily that didn't visit you, as it's the ceiling descender and would have licked your face while you slept! Yuck.

PISHACHA

OTHER NAMES Bishaja, Piśāca

THAILAND

Lost. But when exploring a new country, being lost is not such a bad thing, filling your memories with new images, smells and feelings. Unfortunately, the feelings you are experiencing now are not of wonder but unease. There is a green misty light to the side of the path you are on, and it is curling and rising, changing to a yellowy haze. All around are what look like tall, beautifully carved pepper pots; a landscape of towers like golden beads stacked on top of each other. The glowing vapour moves through the unusual architecture, and you cannot help but follow it. You pass a painted sign written in Thai, which translates as Kanchanaburi Cemetery.

Walking between the ornate graves, you haven't noticed how late it is. You have been following the light for a long time when, from the vapour, a figure emerges. Startled, you begin to say hello, but when it springs forward, you recoil in terror. Its body is covered in bulging veins. Its teeth are too long and sharp to fit in its mouth, and the eyes swell outwards like soft balloons. The eyes! Yellow, glowing and looking directly at you. Just as a scream escapes your mouth, the demon disappears only to reform behind you. Frozen to the spot, you notice more monsters emerging from among the graves. The ghostly lights have delivered you into the clutches of the evil and hungry Pishachas, disgusting demons who love eating people and feeding on human energy.

In Thailand, south-east Asia, these demons feature in folklore and Hindu myths. Haunting cemeteries and dark places, they have many clever tricks to catch their prey. They even speak their own language – Paisāci. Shapeshifting from vile, veiny, yellow-eyed demons to take on any form, they can become invisible and use magic lights, *ignis fatuus*, to trick travellers into straying off their path. Pishachas cause illness and spread disease. To kill them you need a blessed sword, but sadly you forgot to pack one.

MONGOLIAN DEATH WORM

OTHER NAMES Large Intestine Worm, Olgoi-Khorkhoi

MONGOLIA

The Gobi Desert in Mongolia; shifting burning sands, scorching heat; temperatures here are some of the hottest on Earth, where it seems nothing could possibly survive. The air is dry, but the rains eventually roll in around June and July each year. The fat droplets wet the hissing sand and seep down into the cracked earth below.

As the torrential rains fall, waves form on the surface. Great, rippling sand waves, as though there is something other than water moving the desert floor. Cracks form in the golden crust and then ... it appears! Exploding out of the sand, like an immense 1-metre-long red sausage, is the grotesque Mongolian Death Worm! With no real head or legs, it has a round sucker hole with razor-sharp teeth where its face should be. It spits electricity that will kill you! Just one touch of its burnt red skin will kill you! That sucker face will kill you! And its poisonous venom that will kill you too, as well as corrode metal, which will also kill your car!

This worm has only been sighted in the last few decades in Mongolia. From 1990 until 2009 people invested money into expeditions, or monster hunts, desperate to find evidence that the deadly worm exists. Or at least snap a picture of it as they run away screaming.

It's thought that the Mongolian Death Worm lives in a network of tunnels under the desert, only waking to surface during the summer rains. Similarly, normal-sized garden worms do the same, just without venom and electricity. The Mongolian Death Worm may live in a desert oven, but some animals live in far worse places on Earth. Extremophiles, which are organisms that can survive in extreme habitats, love boiling-hot volcanic vents on the sea floor or freezing polar ice. Suddenly, the desert doesn't seem that bad! Will you join the next expedition to find the Mongolian Death Worm? Or are you happy with the normal garden variety?

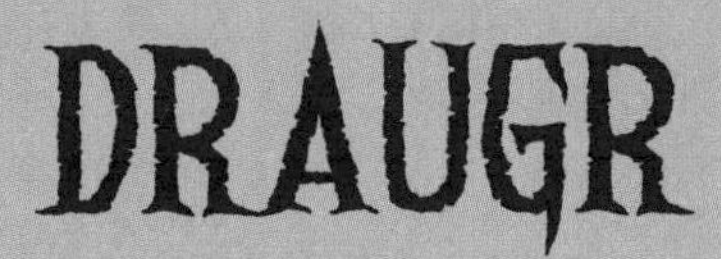

DRAUGR

OTHER NAMES Aptgangr, Draug, Draugen

NORWAY

There is a saying, 'You can never have enough of a good thing', and then you eat a tub of ice cream and have to disagree. How about, 'You can never have enough of a bad thing'? Surely nobody wants a large amount of bad stuff, or do they? Time to introduce you to the Draugr ...

This mythological Norse nightmare monster has survived and spread across Scandinavian countries and into films and video games. The Draugr, or Draugen, are undead, unhappy, unhygienic, unkind, unwelcome bodies that have risen from the grave. They sound like zombies or ghouls, but these monsters have everything on a monster's wish list! EVERYTHING. Fuelled by hatred, their bodies reek of decay and are so incredibly heavy that they can flatten you into a stinking heap. They kill by crushing, drinking blood, sending you insane, or the classic, simply eating you. Their skills make them a boss monster; they can walk through solid objects, make birds fall from the sky, make animals go insane and shapeshift into skinless bulls and horses, seals and cute cats. You might think cute cats don't sound that bad. Well, this cute cat – kattakyn – enters your home and sits on your chest as you sleep, getting heavier and heavier until you die! It doesn't stop there. Draugr can control the weather, causing immense storms at sea that wreck ships. It can also see into the future and turn day into night, and in that awful darkness, it will kill anyone it comes across!

Draugr can even become the reanimated bodies of dead sailors. Their faces are entirely made of seaweed, with just two black eyes, and they wear an oilskin raincoat. During storms, they captain half a wooden rowing boat that can be seen perched on the crest of a wave when it's about to smash your ship into bits. The Draugr are said to be the spirits of all those lost or drowned at sea.

The Draugr makes having too much bad look so good!

DROP BEAR

OTHER NAMES Thylarctos plummetus

AUSTRALIA

Prepare to meet Australia's dangerous national secret! Just koalas on a bad day? No! Never underestimate a Drop Bear. These vicious, meat-eating, coarse-furred marsupials (animals who carry their young in pouches) are as large as leopards and weigh the same as a giant panda. Watch, listen and learn ...

Here, in the dense, forested area of south-east Australia, we see the tourist, not native to this area. It looks like we have caught a glimpse of them following advice from locals to protect themselves from the ferocious Drop Bear. If we observe the tourist closely, we can spot three methods of camouflage that'll defend them from an attack.

Shhh ... Can you hear that noise? It's their terrible impression of an Australian accent. Drop Bears swarm to foreign accents like bees around honey, so this tourist is disguising theirs (badly). Ah, and there, you see the classic dinner-fork-in-the-hair technique that's used to defend from airborne attacks. The use of a plastic fork is a risky substitution though. Now, breathe in that yeasty smell ... they've smeared veggie paste all over their sunburned body to cover the smell of their own nervous sweat.

Now we've seen the prey, can you spot the predator? A Drop Bear will wait in the dense upper foliage of the Australian bush to ambush unprotected passers-by. They wait for hours, before making their signature move, the drop! Small Drop Bears can drop, knock down and bite a tourist. A fully grown Drop Bear can crush a car. It is clear now why the tourist has armed themselves so thoroughly, and successfully, as they continue their holiday untrampled.

Drop Bears are part of contemporary Australian folklore, very popular for scaring visitors. They aren't just for fun though. If you see Beware Drop Bear signs, do not laugh. There are real-life monsters in Australia that will slither, climb and bite you! So be safe and not sorry. And maybe pack a fork, vegetable paste and rehearse your Aussie accent, just in case.

DANGER!

LAKE TIANCHI MONSTER

CHINA AND NORTH KOREA

More than one thousand years ago, there was a violent and spectacular volcanic eruption that exploded Mount Paektu. The volcano, which sits on the border of China and North Korea, was left with a large crater lake, called Heaven Lake or Lake Tianchi. This deep-blue body of water sits high up on the mountain and is covered in ice for nine months of the year. The volcanic lake is a beautiful sight, and people trek up the mountain to marvel at it. But that's not all they come to see! For Lake Tianchi has a secret that lurks in the waters and has been sighted by hundreds of onlookers since 1903.

Down in the sapphire waters, resting on the belly of the active volcano, lives the Lake Tianchi Monster! Or is it Monsters?

In 1903, people reported seeing a large, buffalo-like creature attack people who were on the lake. It had a long neck and smooth, pale-grey skin, like an eel.

More than a hundred people saw 'monsters' fighting in the water in 1962, causing waves on the usually calm lake.

Then in 2007, film footage apparently showed a cluster of monsters. But like most monster footage, it is impossible to tell whether you see ripples, a log, fish, shadows or a prehistoric serpent trapped inside a volcanic lake!

If the Lake Tianchi Monster exists, then it is a master of disguise. Similar to the Loch Ness Monster of Scotland, this creature is thought to be related to dinosaurs. It survives in the freezing-cold, ice-capped lake, submerged in the gloom, only breaking the surface ice to breathe air or catch birds in its jaws. The monster also has to tolerate thousands of visitors to the lake, who stare into the water waiting to glimpse it. But who can blame them? A monster living in a volcanic soup bowl, born out of the chaos of a super-eruption, deserves all the attention it gets.

HIDEBEHIND

USA

Driving through the dense forest roads of the USA, it's a long way to the campsite. Peering into the trees, you can only see past one or two trunks before daylight turns to night. You stop at a petrol station to stretch your legs. An old woman wearing oil-stained overalls approaches, 'You folks lost? Need gas?' You get out and walk towards the trees behind the garage. The air smells sweetly of pine, and unthinkingly, you enter the forest. Something's moving up ahead. What is that? You walk a little further when a hand on your shoulder startles you, 'Don't go in there,' the old woman warns, 'the Hidebehind will get you.' She continues ...

'A group of lumberjacks were logging in that forest. You know lumberjacks are woodsmen, their business is chopping down the huge trees. Four men went into the woods, but only one man came out. He said he saw nothing, just the trees. But one by one, his friends went missing. First there was a noise, and one of the men went to look. Only his axe was found in the pine needles. The next man searched for him and heard rustling. He vanished, too. The last two men searched in near darkness, feeling sure they were being watched. They heard breathing, so one looked behind a tree and never came back. The Hidebehind got them.'

This fearsome and mysterious monster has been blamed for many attacks and the disappearance of loggers and walkers in the USA. It has never actually been seen, but it is thought to be a large and powerful creature with sharp nails. The Hidebehind's favourite food is guts! It likes to grab its victims and drag them to its lair, where it eats them. Alcohol is supposed to repel it. The Hidebehind is possibly the hardest monster to find; perhaps it's always there in plain sight, we just aren't looking properly. Can you see it?

AKHLUT

OTHER NAMES Kăk-whăn'-û-ghăt Kĭg-û-lu'-nĭk

ARCTIC

There once was a man so obsessed with the sea that he was cast out of his village in the Arctic Circle. He joined a pack of wolves, soon becoming one of them, but his love of the water transformed him again, this time from a wolf into an orca. Hungry for revenge on his village, he morphed back into a wolf, eating and punishing his people. If the people were camped on land, his wolf self would drag the victims into the frozen sea. But if anyone fell asleep by the ice edge, then his orca form would rise from the icy Arctic waters and grab them like an orca grabs a seal.

The story of Akhlut is part of the mythology of the Inuit Yup'ik people, who live in Alaska, USA. Sightings of paw prints leading to the water's edge, and wolf tracks coming out of the icy sea and onto land, are all proof of his existence for the Yup'ik people. Akhlut is also known as Kăk-whăn'-û-ghăt Kĭg-û-lu'-nĭk, which translates as 'an orca that changes shape to become a wolf'. Orcas, or killer whales, are also called sea wolves because they hunt in family packs and can tear through seals, dolphins and even attack whales.

It's along the Bering Straits, the sea between Russia and the USA just below the Arctic Circle, that these shapeshifters lurk. They heave themselves out of the glacial waters and transform effortlessly from smooth, monochrome whales into hairy mammals! Both of these animals are top, or apex, predators, as no other animals hunt them. Akhlut is not the only shapeshifting monster from Inuit stories though. There is also a white whale that transforms into a reindeer – not quite as menacing but equally incredible!

These hybrid monsters are visually impressive. They're a bit like the flip books that let you choose different animal heads to match with different animal bodies. What shapeshifting monster would you make? Perhaps a parrot-pig, a horse-snail or a cat-octopus – a catopus! It would be hard to create one fiercer than Akhlut, though.

HO TINH

OTHER NAMES Huli Jing

VIETNAM

Vietnam, in south-east Asia, is populated with almost 100 million people. It has stunning scenery, deep mysterious caves, a bridge held up by giant stone hands and lanterns that float on its blue waters every full moon. It also has a mythical creature that once terrorised the people of the country, especially around Long Bien, in northern Vietnam.

According to legend, people of the area were being attacked at night, but the only sound that they heard was a baby crying. People were terrified of this unknown threat and locked themselves in their homes.

Deep in a cave, not far from the town, was a beautiful woman surrounded by piles of bones and other monstrous leftovers. Nesting swifts and stalactites covered the ceiling, below which she sat eating her latest victim.

There were more disappearances, and the town was paralysed with fear, but then Lac Long Quan, the Dragon Lord of Lac and father of the Vietnamese people, arrived. He set about finding this unseen monster. He was already a heroic figure who, according to another legend, made 100 eggs with his wife that hatched the first Vietnamese people, who were then split between the land and the sea.

One day while out hunting the monster, Quan met a beautiful woman. Charming and courteous, she lured him to a cave – yes, that cave. Intrigued, he went with her, but once inside, she transformed. Twisting and screaming, she became a golden fox with nine tails. A fight to the death began. The fox, known as Ho Tinh, wanted meat, and Quan wanted safety for his people. Eventually, Quan raised his sword and cut off the fox's head. Temples were raised to honour him.

China's Huli Jing, Korea's Kumiho and Japan's Kitsune are all versions of the nine-tailed fox monster. If you hear a baby cry in the night, look outside, and if you see a fox with nine tails then quickly lock your door.

IKUJI

OTHER NAMES Ayakashi

JAPAN

For every season, emotion and situation, Japan has a monster. Weird and beautiful, they are known as *yokai*. They animate people's fears, act as warnings and some, like the never-ending Ikuji, teach important life lessons.

Imagine drawing a chalk line from your front door, along the street, through town, past fields and on for three hours. You have drawn the length of Ikuji! Three hours long, slithering in the oceans off Japan.

Now let's travel back more than 150 years, to a time in Japan known as the Edo period. The oily sea serpent, Ikuji, is terrorising Japan's turbulent fishing waters.

Sailors report different encounters with this monster. Some only spot a coil of its body. Others say they feel a violent jolt as it passes close by, like an eerie underwater skyscraper. But when Ikuji raises its head to look upon a boat that's in its path, it sparks panic and terror. Because Ikuji must slither OVER the boat. The huge, sickly slick body pumps out slime as it goes, filling the deck to the brim with glowing muck. It oozes between deck planks, loosens bolts and soaks sails, squishing between toes and coating everything it touches. After three hours, Ikuji leaves the boat as full of slime as a bath is full of water.

For hours, by lamplight, the crew must work to save the boat from sinking. Heaving buckets of slime overboard, scraping ooze from wood and canvas, slipping and falling as they go. They cannot stop to daydream or rest. The lesson of Ikuji is simple: if you work hard together, harder than you can imagine and work efficiently, you won't join the lazy spirits in the waters below. Ikuji lets you live to tell the tale.

So, if you refuse to tidy your room, imagine Ikuji filling everywhere with slime so fast you think you will surely perish. Ikuji is a warning to the lazy. Work hard. Live long!

DULLAHAN

OTHER NAMES **Dullaghan, Gan Ceann, Headless Horseman**

IRELAND

Halloween, All Hallows Eve, when costumed trick-or-treaters knock on doors, grab sweets and eat them under ghost sheets and werewolf masks. Pumpkins are scooped out and carved with jagged mouths and triangular eyes. Doorsteps glow with their evil grimaces.

The Dullahan has his own pumpkin. His is no doorstep decoration for Halloween, but rather a replacement for his severed head! Ireland's ghoulish, mythological Dullahan, or Headless Horseman, is a horrifying sight. The horseman rides a large black stallion and where once he had a head, now only a raw stump of neck can be seen. His real head is sometimes carried under one arm, and its bloodshot eyes roll around like wet marbles in their sockets. In other stories, he holds a lit pumpkin instead of a head! He cracks a whip made of human spines, glowing white in the moonlight, as he gallops looking for his next victim. You never want to hear those hooves approach or see the burning lantern eyes, not even at Halloween. If Dullahan stops his horse near to you, if he calls out your name, you are doomed! He is a death bearer; he rides to collect souls.

You could find something made of gold, because Dullahan is terrified of gold. It is not known why, but it seems to repel him.

The Dullahan is featured in Washington Irving's novel *The Legend of Sleepy Hollow*, which has become the most popular version of the Dullahan myth, made into cartoons and films. *Sleepy Hollow*'s horseman has the classic pumpkin head, which has become so well known, and links the myth to Halloween.

Pumpkin head lanterns, also called Jack o' Lanterns in the USA, started in Ireland and were originally made from hollowed-out turnips and displayed to ward off evil spirits. They are now part of Halloween tradition across the world. There is even the Jack o' Lantern Nebula, a star cluster that resembles the Dullahan's replacement head!

BLACK SHUCK

OTHER NAMES Old Shock, Old Shuck

ENGLAND

It's a beautiful day for a picnic. While on holiday in Norfolk, you munch your sandwich and flick away the ants trying to steal cake crumbs. You look up at the weathered Norman towers of Bungay Castle, when all of a sudden you are flattened by a black dog, and a sloppy tongue licks your face! 'I am so sorry ...' a woman runs up to pull her black Labrador off you. 'I love dogs,' you laugh, as you wipe your face. 'Not all dogs though,' she says. 'Yes, even picnic intruders!' you insist, as you stroke the dog's head. 'Not Black Shuck.' the woman says. With those words, the sun disappeared behind a black cloud and thunder rumbles.

Black Shuck is the demon hellhound of East Anglia! Famous in local folklore, it's been sighted since the 1500s. A huge, fierce dog, with blood-red eyes, or a single eye on its forehead, and paws that make no sound. It lets out blood-curdling howls and is the documented killer of innocent people in Norfolk and Suffolk.

In 1577, in St Mary's Church in Bungay, two people were praying when a deafening roar and the smell of burning was followed by a huge demon hound bursting into the church. It ran over the pews, mauling the two people to death! All that was left was a burnt door and a partly destroyed church! The same had happened in Suffolk earlier that year. Pamphlets were printed warning of the 'Strange and Terrible Wonder'. People were terrified.

What could it be, if not an evil hellhound with no respect for the lives of innocent people? Black dogs are common in myths and legends. They attract superstitions and are creatures of evil in folklore. The churches involved in the attacks had signs of lightning strikes. Scorch marks showed how electricity had hit the steeples. There are also huge dog breeds, such as Newfoundlands and Irish Wolfhounds. Who knows if Black Shuck still prowls the churchyards in Norfolk, but at least the sun has come back out and you can eat your cake.

COLÔROBÈTCH

OTHER NAMES Colo Rodje Betch, Red Beak, Routge Betch

BELGIUM AND FRANCE

Hoed. Handschoenen. Sjaal! Chapeau. Gants. Echarpe! Mütze. Handschuhe. Schal!

Every child in Belgium hears these vital three words – Hat. Gloves. Scarf! – over and over again in the three languages that Belgians speak, Dutch, French and German. Boring! What's the big deal if it's cold, you get chilly hands and face. It's nothing to cry about!

Oh, but it is ... On 28 February 2018, Elsenborn in Belgium experienced a record low temperature of -18°C! That would leave some incredibly cold fingers and toes. Let's hope the children listened to the hat, gloves and scarf advice because something is lurking out there, something that hopes beyond hope that you have forgotten your knitwear.

The icy wind and dropping temperature don't just blanket the fields with frost and make your breath cloudy. It also calls to a monstrous creature whose staple diet is frozen flesh, cold noses, frost-nipped fingers and wind-chilled ears. Colôrobètch is coming. You can hear the tinkling of its ice feathers. It has a rooster's head on an emu-sized body. Doesn't sound that scary, does it? How about its human face, which is stretched open by a sharp, blood-red beak that's red from pecking at its victims' frozen skin?

You can't see the Colôrobètch, but it will follow chilly children home as they clap their cold hands for warmth and pull up their coat collar after forgetting their woollens. First it will start with frost nip, pecking gently at the exposed skin. Then it moves on to mild frostbite, causing pain, redness and split skin. Finally, black, dead skin. Snapping and breathing its icy breath, it freezes all the exposed yummy bits so it can nibble off the frozen flesh!

From the folktales of France and Belgium, Colôrobètch is used to scare children into being sensible in the cold. The human bird with its icicle feathers collects stray gloves as it hunts for more victims. Designed to protect and teach, it certainly makes you grab those mittens before leaving the house!

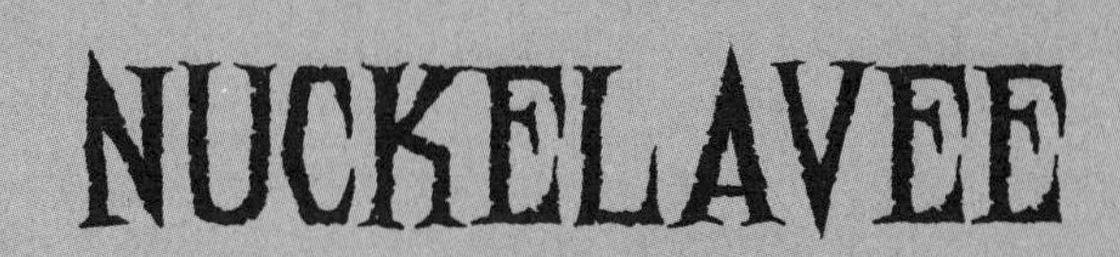

NUCKELAVEE

SCOTLAND

'Tammas, calm yourself!' The farmer comforted the distressed man who had run into his farmhouse. Tammas looked ragged, chalk white and was sweating, his clothing soaked from wading in the river. 'What is wrong? Drink this,' Tammas sipped the hot ale. He seemed calmer. 'It's coming, we're doomed!' he began ...

'I was on the beach this night, digging for fishing bait and scratching about for seaweed. The sea was wild, screaming at me and the clouds blew in fast. There was no one about. I had a clear head; I am not mad. I noticed hoof prints in the sand and the shore plants were blackened as though fire had ripped through them. There was a reek and stench all around. I made to go back home, but something blocked the path. It, it ...'

'Go on, Tammas.'

'It was the, I must not say it, it was the Devil of the Sea that stood in front of me! A horse and rider but joined as one. Long arms dragged on the ground, the rider's head was large and bloated and the horse had only one big, burning eye that stared at me. The thing had no skin or coat, just wet red veins all over its two bodies. On opening its mouth a black fog billowed out, the stench killed the trees and grasses, almost reaching me. I ran! It followed! Burning a trail; cattle fell dead and I almost did, but as I waded across the river it stopped. It could not stand the river! It stood and stared at me as I screamed.'

That was the first eyewitness of the Nuckelavee, a vile monster from the islands of Orkney, in Scotland. No Orcadian – a person from the Orkney islands – may speak its name. This creature emerged from Norse legends, from a time when people from Scandinavian once inhabited Scotland. The Nuckelavee was blamed for plagues and failed crops on the islands. Freshwater is its only fear, rain and rivers will repel it. Tammas had a very lucky escape!

CRABZILLA

ENGLAND

It's a sizzling summer day on the pebbly shores of Whitstable, a small fishing town on the Kent coast, in the south of England. These days must be cherished as the weather can change its mind at any second and rain on your fish and chips! The view is of a green sea, wind farm turbines that turn like the colourful pinwheels you can blow, and far off, there's the old rusting sea forts with only seals for company.

Two boys are crabbing on the jetty. Their clear bucket is filled with sea water, and the crab line is baited with bits of old fish. They lie on their stomachs dangling the long line into the seaweed-darkened depths. The line gently tugs; they wait for another tug and then draw the line up carefully. Yes! There are at least six crabs attached, nipping and clacking. In the bucket they fight with each other. The boys get a close-up look at the amazing crab anatomy.

The line tugs and pulls again so the boys start to draw it up, but it's stuck. They yank it, frustrated, and what rises up sends their screams out across the North Sea and probably as far as Amsterdam! A humongous orange claw rises up, as tall as boat sails, and then the sea drains away as the shell of this monstrous crustacean surfaces! On the beach someone clicks a photo of this terrifying scene. Behold the rise of Crabzilla, the 15-metre-wide, 450-kilogram giant crab of Whitstable Bay!

In 2013, an aerial photo surfaced showing what appeared to be a crab at least five cars wide near the jetty. The image drew worldwide attention, and newspapers headlined with CRABZILLA! Surely a hoax? Zoologists pointed out that a crab this size would be impossible as it would weigh as much as a sailboat. The largest and heaviest known crabs are the Tasmanian giant crab and the Japanese spider crab. The Japanese spider crab grows to a measly 4 metres long – a baby in the shadow of this shelly monstrosity!

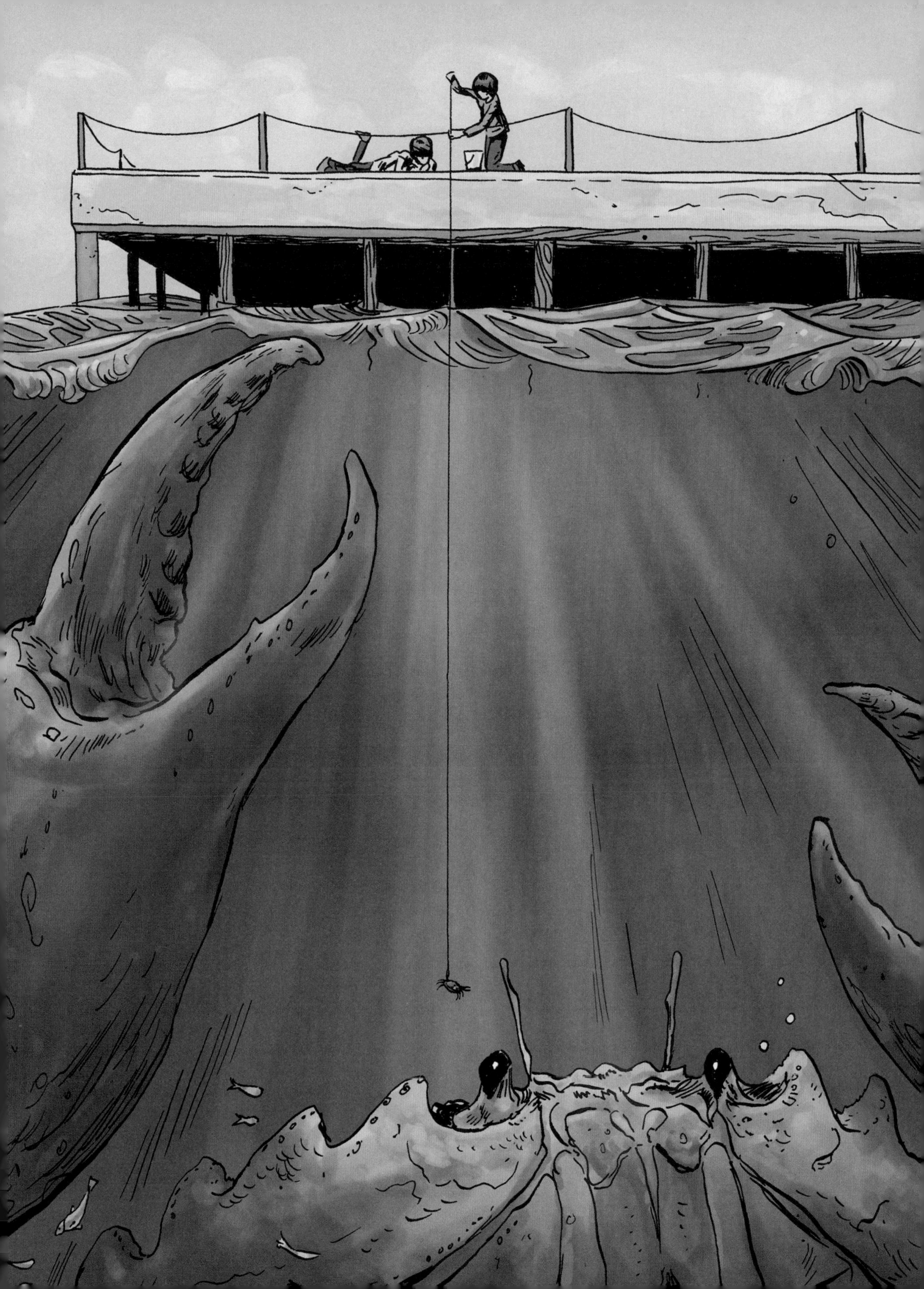

FROST GIANT

OTHER NAMES Isejötunen, Jötunn

ICELAND AND NORWAY

Icebergs are just the visible peaks of much greater ice mountains that hide below the surface of the sea. From above they appear blue, as ice scatters blue light waves and absorbs the other colours, leaving an intense sky-blue. These giant ice chunks may have influenced descriptions of the mighty Frost Giants, or Jötunn, from Norse sagas, stories written in the thirteenth and fourteenth centuries from Iceland and Norway. Frost Giants were a warring and troublemaking race of blue-skinned people created from the underarm sweat of Ymir. That detail may need an explanation ...

According to legend, Ymir was made from melting ice and intense heat, and he grew male and female Frost Giants from his sweat, as well as a six-legged son from his own leg! He was killed in order to create a mythical Norse world, and the Frost Giants sailed to safety on the flood made from his blood!

Frost Giants lived in the mythical land of Jötunheimr and were a powerful race who were sometimes seen as giants. They disagreed with the Norse gods and fought with Odin, the god of war. The Frost Giants lived in castles and caves and were as blue, strong and solid as the glacial icebergs. Loki is perhaps the most famous Frost Giant, who you may recognise from the Marvel Thor and Avengers films. He is the god of mischief and trickery and can hide his Frost Giant appearance by taking on the look of anyone he chooses.

Frost Giants are not so much ice monsters as ice warriors, with freezing water coursing through their veins. Humans are sixty per cent water, so perhaps we're not so different from these Norse legends. There are many ice monsters far more dangerous and disturbing from around the world. The best are probably the Inuit creations from the Arctic regions: Ijiraq, the half-human half-caribou monster and Mahaha, the grinning, long-nailed monster that tickles you to death, leaving you a grinning icy corpse! At least Frost Giants don't tickle!

VAMPIRE

OTHER NAMES Nachzehrer, Striga, Vrykolakas

WORLDWIDE

Are you feeling peaky? Pale, ghastly complexion? Are you always hungry but don't fancy your sandwiches? And your spaghetti bolognese, is it too garlicky? Lost your reflection in the mirror? Can't go into your friend's house without being invited across the threshold? Sunlight make you explode? Prefer to stay indoors and sleep in a soil-filled box in the basement instead? Transform easily into a bat? Hypnotise people by staring at them? And your pulse, has that stopped too? I do believe you've come down with something, but it isn't a cold: you are a vampire!

Hundreds of years of folklore and superstition have seen these bloated undead beings, who rise from their coffins and terrorise towns, turn into the vampires we recognise today. It was only in the nineteenth century that these vile, shrouded things became the Dracula type of vampire we know so well. In 1897, Bram Stocker wrote his famous novel *Dracula,* about the vampire Count who travels to England by ship, feeding on the crew and then the people of Whitby. He was charismatic, mesmerising and deadly.

Blood-drinking creatures have long haunted monster mythology. And blood, death, graverobbing and disease were all very real problems for people from the 1700s. Vampire attacks seemed to explain misunderstood illnesses and unexplained deaths. Bodies found with blood around the mouth in coffins usually showed the person had a particular disease, but at the time, scientists couldn't explain these things.

But it doesn't hurt to protect yourself just in case you do meet a vampire. Gather together a small collection of household items: garlic, hawthorn twigs, wild roses, a holy cross, rosary beads and holy water. Then stay near to some running water, vampires can't cross running water. And just in case these all let you down, a nice sharp wooden stake to drive into the vampire's heart should do it. Remember though, do not invite them in, no matter how polite you are or however charming they seem, just don't.

KAMAITACHI

OTHER NAMES Kama Itachi, Qiongqi, Sickle Weasel

JAPAN

Beware the Kamaitachi!

As you travel along the mountain track in the Koshin'etsu region of Japan, the wind playfully catches your coat and ruffles your hair. Up here the mountain winds can whip and wail. Ahead you see dust spirals are forming in the dirt like tiny, devilish tornadoes. You stop, sensing something is watching you. Suddenly, the sun goes in and the temperature drops. You hear high-pitched barks and the dust devils grow, whipping you with leaves and pebbles. You start to run, but it's too late! The first twister catches your legs, ouch, it scratches you! You stumble as the second gust sharply whips you again. Just as you try to get up, another spiral rolls over you. What was that?! Why are you covered in small paw prints ...?

You've been a victim of the Kamaitachi, or Sickle Weasels! These invisible Japanese monsters ride on the cold winds, always travelling in threes. They have curved knives, called sickles, for hands and feet, weasel faces, fur-like hedgehog spines and they bark. Riding small tornadoes, the first weasel cuts your legs so you fall down, the second cuts your hands and face! Oh no, what is the third one going to do?! The third weasel gently treats your cuts with magic cream to heal them. Well, that was a surprise.

The Kamaitachi are related to another mischievous Japanese weasel, the Itachi, who have different tricks. Itachi will stand on each other's shoulders in a weasel column and make fire tornadoes, which can set alight towns. These creatures are naughty with a capital 'N'.

Kamaitachi and Itachi exist in Japanese culture to teach lessons: wear warm clothes in the cold, and be careful of careless fires and cute animals. If you think about how painful the winter wind is on ungloved hands after throwing snowballs, you can imagine how the idea of knife-wielding weasels came about. Almost.

ARABIAN GHOUL

OTHER NAMES Ghul

ARABIA

There are a list of interests that seem to be popular, almost necessary, for many of the monsters within this book. But just because they are popular, it doesn't make them any less disgusting! You may have a list of interests; perhaps reading, playing football, dancing or playing an instrument. These are fun, healthy and will make your life happier.

Now let us take a look at the Arabian Ghoul's interests. Perhaps she will love dancing or playing rugby at weekends?

Let's see, likes to lurk in dimly lit cemeteries. Well, she could be passionate about history? She loves to dig up graves with her sharp claws, and when she has discovered the grave's inhabitant, she likes to eat them. Oh dear. This interest is called cannibalism, and it's both revolting and illegal. She likes to ride on the backs of large hares and dogs. This isn't too strange, but it's pretty unusual. She also has a dangerous habit of setting fires just off the side of paths, luring passers-by so she can eat them! We can clearly see that the Arabian Ghoul is a disgusting creature and also, she needs new hobbies.

All of these interests have meant that ghouls have been feared in Arabian folklore since the eighth century. Stories tell of their vile habits and cruelty. They're depicted as undead, demonic and monstrous jinns (spirits) with rotting bodies. But unlike Zombies, they can think for themselves, so they can scheme and trap their victims.

The Arabian Ghoul's cousin, the English Ghoul, appeared 1,000 years later in stories from the eighteenth century, where it became a popular classic monster alongside vampires, zombies and werewolves. The idea of these dead creatures feeding on the living, never resting peacefully and haunting gravesites is such a popular monster characteristic. These monsters draw out our fears and allow us to share them with others in the form of stories.

AQRABUAMELU

OTHER NAMES Girtablilu, Scorpion Men

IRAN, IRAQ AND SYRIA

There is no doubt that if you were designing a monster that was part-animal part-human, you could do no better than sticking a scorpion tail on it! Scorpions look superbly deadly, with their outer skeleton of separated armour and the venomous tail arched over their back. They have glow-in-the-dark special effects and the ability to survive almost anything – these are top predators and deadly, ancient creatures.

Look upon the powerful scorpion men, Aqrabuamelu! They were the armoured gatekeepers to the Babylonian Underworld – the land of the dead. Babylon was an ancient city in Mesopotamia, which existed more than 4,000 years ago. This area is now modern-day Iraq, Iran and Syria, in the Middle East, but back then it was ruled by the religious empire of the Akkadians. The Babylonians believed that the Aqrabuamelu insect monsters stood proudly before the sacred twin-peaked mountain of Mashu. The mountain was both home to the gods and the entrance to the Underworld. The Aqrabuamelu would open and close the gates for the sun god Shamesh, so he could rise and fall, setting each day in motion. These half-man half-scorpion giants were the perfect guards. Armed with bows and arrows, they could touch the sky and had a stare that could kill!

Other cultures have similar scorpion creatures; Hedetet and Serket are half-scorpion goddesses from ancient Egypt, and Tzitzimime are Aztec scorpion men.

Scorpions are exquisite survivors. Their 400-million-year-old fossil relatives are thought to be some of the first sea creatures that survived on land. Some scorpions have deadly venom, such as the deathstalker scorpion, found in the Middle East. The largest scorpions are the length of a ruler, but some are tiny enough to hide in your shoe!

Imagine those eight strong legs running after you on the hot sands, their two pedipalps – pincers – clicking and the barbed tail darting to strike. Now imagine the Aqrabuamelu grabbing you with those pincers! These creatures are monstrous without human bodies attached, but as a mythical beast they are unstoppable!

SIDEHILL GOUGER

OTHER NAMES Cutter Cuss, Hoofer, Rickaboo Racker

USA

Class settle down! Say 'yes' when I call your name: Cutter Cuss – 'yes', Gudaphro – 'yes', Gwinter – 'yes', Gyascutus – 'yes', Hunkus, Hunkus? – 'yes', Prock – 'yes', Rickaboo Racker – 'yes', Sidehill Dodger – 'yes', Sidehill Gouger – 'yes', Sidehill Hoofer – 'yes', Sidehill Loper – 'yes', Sidehill Ousel – 'yes', Sidewinder – 'yes', Wampahoofus – 'yes', Wampus – 'yes'! All present and not quite correct, for this is a class of just one incredibly bizarre student, the Sidehill Gouger. Let's leave the classroom and take a trip to a steep mountainside in Wisconsin, USA ...

Hunkered down on a rocky edge, we are waiting to see the curious occupant of a burrow just ahead ... There, do you see, a Sidehill Gouger has stepped out of the burrow mouth. It is facing away from us and walking incredibly smoothly, which is amazing as it is impossible to move well on this very steep hillside. A sound has startled it, and it has stopped moving. Now, it seems to be trying to turn around, but it can't because both legs on one side of its body are short and the other two legs are long! Oh no, it has rolled down the mountain! It looks unhurt, but it's now just walking in circles, like a maths compass!

Sidehill Gougers are a ridiculous folklore creation. According to the stories, they are mammals who lay eggs – which mammals rarely do! – and their legs have adapted so they can walk on steep mountainsides. There have been many sightings of these lopsided creatures, who look quite normal walking on the side of hills, but very strange going in circles on flat ground. Some say they are pig-like, others goaty, or cow-like or deer-like. But all say they are utterly silly.

Apparently, the first gougers, known as Wampahoofuses or Wampahoofi, walked all the way from New England to Wisconsin, USA, leaning on each other for balance!

CHUPACABRA

OTHER NAMES Grunches

PUERTO RICO

Twenty years ago, on the outskirts of a small Puerto Rican town, a goat farmer witnesses a monstrous attack …

It is a cold and clear night. The goats are safely locked up in their wooden sheds. Their breath clouds as they jostle together, jangling their bells softly. The sound of cricket-like cicadas fill the darkness, and clouds drift across the nearby mountains. When suddenly, the shed's metal roof makes a deafening clang and bends as something lands on it. The goats startle, staring with their strange rectangular pupils, they bleat loudly. The thing on the roof growls as it moves along the thin metal panels. The goats smell the creature's stench, making them squeal and fret. Then, the wooden doors to the shed are ripped off and there is a snarling roar as the infamous Chupacabra enters, like a toothed bowling ball hurled at the goats, causing mayhem.

The farmer, woken, stumbles into the yard and shines his torch beam onto his shed. In the light he sees a bear-sized monster with huge spines on its back and sharp teeth in its open mouth. '*¡Chupacabra!*' he whispers, '*¡Chupacabra! ¡No, mis cabras! ¡Mis pobres cabras!*'

This infamous creature, only sighted since 1995, has been blamed for cattle deaths in Puerto Rico, in the Caribbean. Sightings have described the animal as reptilian, or dog-like or even alien-like. It leaves strange three-hole bite marks and drinks the animals' blood. There have been reported sightings in the USA, Chile, Philippines and as far away as Russia. A monster can be relatively new in folklore, but its reputation can still travel like wildfire.

Chupacabras may simply be Mexican hairless dogs or starving coyotes with an infection called mange, which causes hair loss. Coarse hair along their backs perhaps looks like spines? But one thing's for sure, something is killing the goats. ¡Pobres cabras! Poor goats!

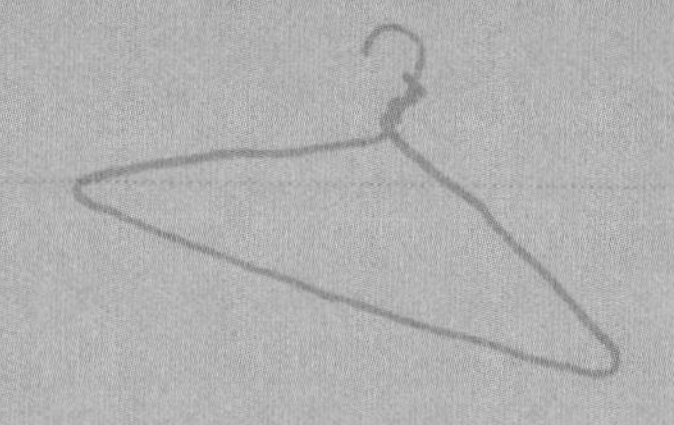

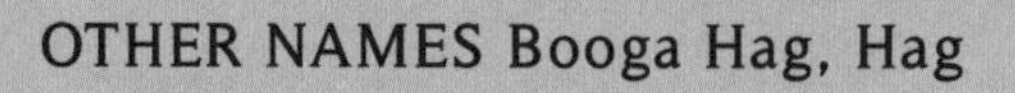

BOO-HAG

OTHER NAMES Booga Hag, Hag

USA

'Boo-Hag comin' to get me, Oh no, she won't leave me alone, The doctor tell me to trick her, Put a pair of brooms by the bed, Boo-Hag ain't gonna steal my breath, She got to count the straws instead!'

This blues lullaby was sung to sleepy children in Georgia, Florida and North and South Carolina, in the USA. In Gullah culture, African-American communities found in the southern states, this was a bedtime favourite. Imagine being lulled to sleep imagining the Boo-Hag coming to visit you …

It's bedtime in Cape Fear, North Carolina, and it is hot. A creaky fan squeaks and wobbles above the bed. Out on the front porch, moths beat against the light, which shines on the wet, naked, red thing standing at the door. Boo-Hag rattles the handle, leaving behind red, sticky fingerprints. Through a hole in the doorframe she pushes, squeezing her body liquidly into the house. Quietly, she squelches to the bedroom. It's here she will begin to feed. She may be red, but she doesn't want blood, it's your breath she's after, and maybe your skin too. She puts you into a deep dream-filled sleep and steals your breath, not all of it, just enough to fill her up. That is unless you wake up and see her. If you catch sight of Boo-Hag, she will take your skin and wear it like a new dress! Oh dear, you have been 'hagridden'. By placing a broom by your bed you would have been protected, as Boo-Hag cannot help but count the bristles and forget all about you.

The Boo-Hag is part of the folklore hag characters that include vile witches and old women. She is able to unzip her skin and fly in her red, skinless state. If only Boo-Hag had the Internet, she could order her clothes online rather than bother with stealing skin! Instead, she can only stare longingly at shop window displays in the dead of night dreaming of her perfect outfit!

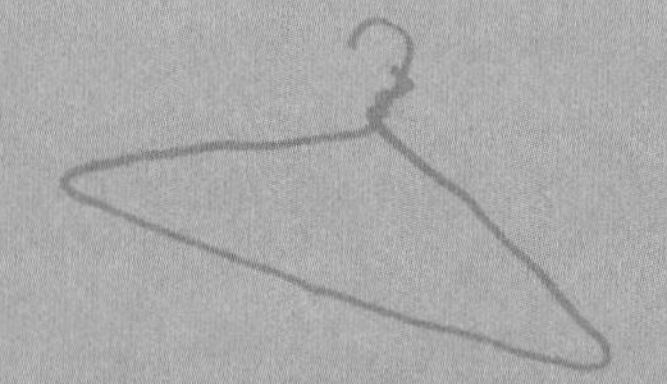

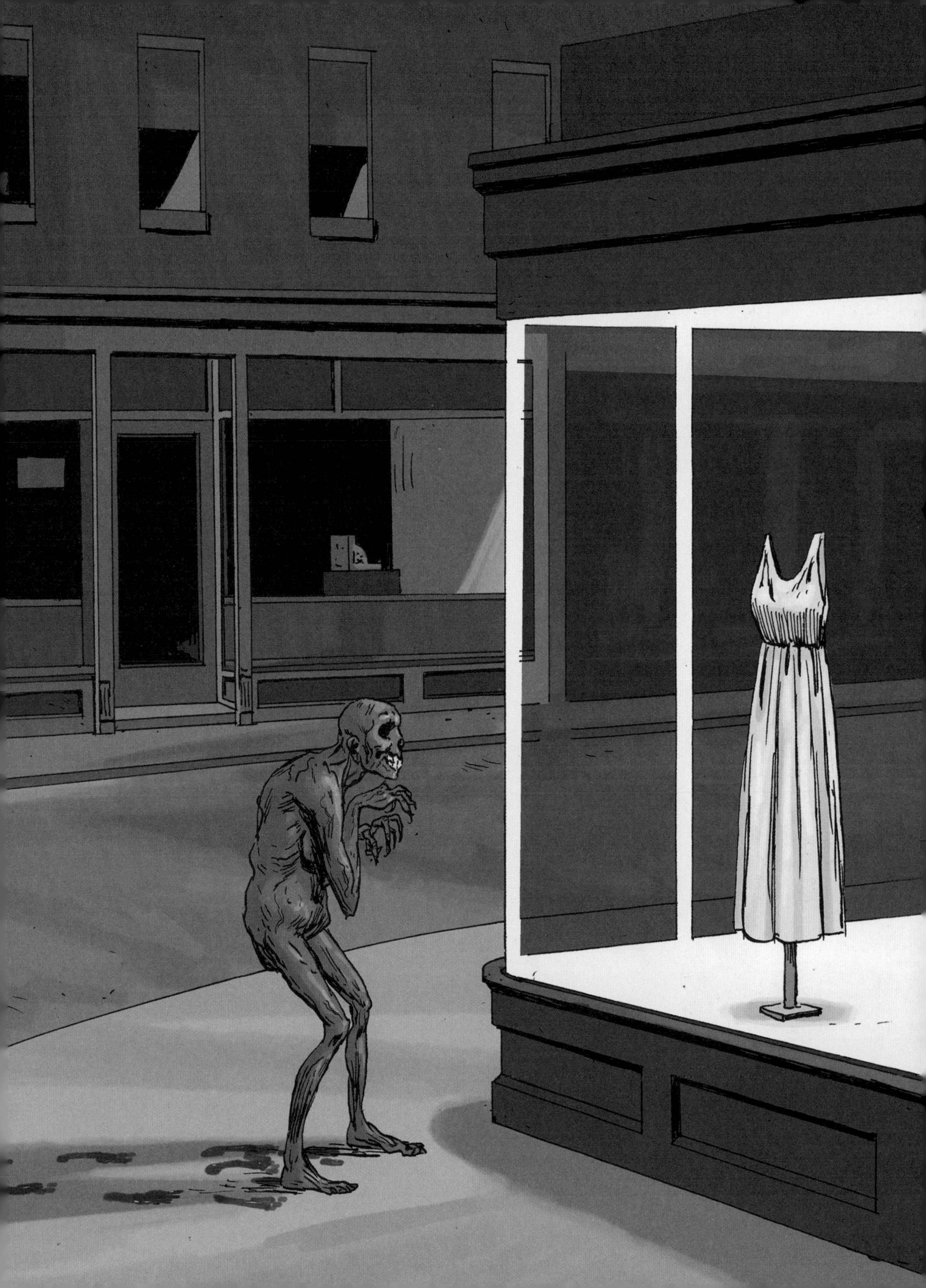

ADAMASTOR

PORTUGAL AND SOUTH AFRICA

Untameable! Unbelievable! Unconquerable! Unimaginable! All of the 'uns' apply to the might, the power and the rage of Adamastor, a fictional giant who created land and conjures up storms.

Adamastor is huge. You may see him hidden in the storm clouds, with his full beard and grotesque, sunken eyes so hollow and sad. His open, screaming mouth becomes the black night sky and his yellowing teeth are the jagged rocks on the shore. When sailors look up at a towering storm while at sea, they scream 'Oh, Adamastor, we are doomed!' On calmer days, his body becomes caves, land, sandstone and the granite of the Cape of Good Hope, in South Africa, where the Indian Ocean meets the Atlantic Ocean.

During the Age of Discovery, in the fifteenth and sixteenth centuries, Portuguese explorers made many attempts to pass this storm-ravaged and dangerous headland while they tried to find a route to Asia around the coast of Africa. It was called *Cabo das Tormentas*, or the Cape of Storms, and many ships were smashed onto the rocks during these attempts. Eventually, Christopher Columbus and Vasco da Gama, the famous explorers, put Portugal on the world map by navigating new routes to India and the Americas. Their bravery and persistence calmed the tormented Adamastor, who eventually let them pass.

Where does this giant come from? A classic Greek myth? Is he an ancient Norse god? No, he comes from the imagination of the Portuguese poet Luis de Camões, who wrote a poem featuring this lovesick giant in 1572. The name Adamastor means untamed, and his story is one of trickery and love. Adamastor was about to marry the woman of his dreams, Tethis, when her mother, a sea goddess, hid Adamastor's bride and tricked him into marrying a rock instead. His fury, heartbreak and confusion changed him into the vast raging titan whose sorrow conjured storms.

Had you ever wondered why the sea is so salty? It is filled with the tears of Adamastor!

TARANTASIO

ITALY

In this place a vast lake once swelled, sickly green was the water and putrid was the smoke that rose from its surface. Gerundo Lake covered the land where the cities of Milan, Bergamo, Lodi and Cremona, in the Lombardy region, now stand. It was a volcanic lake, sitting on top of one of Italy's largest gas deposits. Bubbling and sulphuric, the water would have been too toxic for natural life to thrive, but perfect for mythical beasts to grow in ...

In the lake's dank depths slithered a dragon serpent who carried disease and had a huge appetite. Leaving its lair, it would savagely attack and kill Italian people during the twelfth and thirteenth centuries.

This giant, lake-dwelling dragon was called Tarantasio, and his fame is captured in carvings, crests and even on a football team logo. Legends vary as to who eventually slayed the creature. Was it Visconti, Barbarrossa or Saint Christopher? Nobody can agree, but the dragon is no longer prowling the lush area around Gerundo or spreading the Yellow Plague and eating children.

If you go to the church of San Bassiano in Pizzighettone and look up at the ceiling, you will see a supposed bone from Tarantasio. It's a physical reminder of the vastness of this creature and the fact that he was triumphed over. On closer inspection the bone is probably a fossilised whale bone, but who needs a closer look?

Long after the dragon perished, on an autumn evening, people crowd on a bridge outside Milan to see a monster rise from the depths of the river. Their phones are ready to photograph the furious Tarantasio as it surfaces. Excitement, not fear, ripples over the onlookers as a voice announces he is rising! A giant holographic image of a dragon flickers and sparkles in the water, its reflection as real as the original would have been! How do you think the original beast would feel about people clapping and cheering his name, rather than running screaming in terror from it?

BASAJAUN

OTHER NAMES Lord of the Woods

FRANCE AND SPAIN

It was 1993, in the ruins of an old church in the Pyrenees mountains, a group of cavers saw something that none of them would ever forget. A human-sized creature, covered in dense matted cream-coloured hair that hid most of its face. It was squealing and screaming as it bound through the church rubble.

A young girl hiking with her family in 2011 captured a photograph of a creature on a hillside in Artikutza, Spain. The image shows a large man covered in hair, and the media started to call it the Basque Bigfoot, or Pyrenees Yeti. But this region has its own wild-man myth – Basajaun.

In the western Pyrenees, on the border of south-west France and northern-central Spain, is the Basque country, land where the Basque people have lived for centuries. If you look about the landscape in this area, you will see piles of stones stacked upwards and in circles, called megaliths. There are around eighty in the region, existing since Neanderthals – early relatives of modern humans – roamed the area before dying out some 40,000 years ago. According to the myth, Basajaun taught people how to make these megaliths, as well as craft axes, forage for food, raise crops and care for animals. Basajaun even warned people when storms were near or if their sheep were threatened by wolves. It would scare away predators and was a fierce protector of nature.

Neanderthals shared their skills with modern humans, the Homo sapiens, who eventually succeeded them to thrive and spread. There have been tales of this creature throughout the history of the Basque people. The male is known as Basajaun, Basajaunak if there are more than one and Basandere if female. But who is this Lord of the Woods, and is it friendly or fiendish? Its cream hair was so thick that only its eyes were usually visible, but they were not the eyes of a savage hunter, they held knowledge and a conscience.

BEAST OF EXMOOR

ENGLAND

Cliffs, wilderness, streams, woods, moors, valleys and farms all stretch across 690 square kilometres of Exmoor National Park, in south-west England. Surely within this vast, rugged and changeable scenery, a mystery could stay hidden for a few decades? A mystery in the shape of a large phantom feline!

The folklore and legends of this place tell of a big cat that roams the moors at night, killing cattle and disappearing like a supernatural predator. Since the 1970s, big cats have been sighted in this area and across the moors of the south-west. In 1983, a farmer lost 100 sheep to a throat-biting creature, and word spread that there were wild cats living out in the dark patches of moor, hiding in old mines or rocky dens. Photographs of what can only be described as a large cat, maybe a black puma or panther, by roadsides, on rocky ledges and on the moor caught people's imagination! How could wild cats roam England when apparently the most dangerous animals in the UK are cows!

Around sixty years ago, a law was passed banning people from owning exotic big cats. This led to a handful of irresponsible people releasing their illegal big cats into the wild. Many were captured and rehomed in zoos or destroyed. But could a few be living and breeding on the moors of Devon and Cornwall, as Bodmin in Cornwall also has its own beast sightings?

Coming face to face with a big cat on the moor would be heart-stoppingly scary. The strongest big cat is the panther, and the puma can run up to 80 kilometres an hour and is almost 1.6 metres long. In 1988, the Royal Marines were called in to find the Beast of Exmoor. They did not succeed, but reported tracking a highly intelligent 'creature' who was excellent at evading them. Despite rewards offered and numerous sightings, the big cat has never been found. It remains part of the local legend, prowling the English wilderness.

AFRICAN-RIVER-TOURS

NKALA

ZAMBIA

You are in a cloud! Everything is misty, and there's a roar so loud you feel like you are standing on the wing of a jet. But you are on land. Sort of ... The river tour boat is taking you, and fellow tourists, as near to Victoria Falls as you can be. Found in southern Africa on the border between Zambia and Zimbabwe, it's one of the world's most impressive waterfalls. Also known as Mosi-oa-Tunya, or 'Smoke that Thunders', the air all around you clouds with water vapour. Looking up, the crashing water falls deafeningly into the Zambezi River. Wow. Everyone's raincoat-shaped shadows look strange in the mist.

Somewhere on the boat a tour attendant shouts, you cannot hear over the thundering falls, but he shouts again and again. 'Nkala! Nkala!' You don't understand, but everyone is pointing up at the steep cliff beside the river. In the mist and sunlight, through rainbow-coloured prisms, you see a large rock hanging over the cliff. 'Nkala!' the attendants shout, 'Stay down!' Everyone panics and screams. You feel strange, then you notice that the shadows of the scurrying passengers are rising like smoke in the water haze, yours too. They are being sucked toward the large rock. But that is no rock, it has a face, or faces, and a large body. Looking closer, you see it's a huge crab with two hippopotamus' heads! And they are sucking in the shadows as if drinking milkshakes through a straw!

Nkala is the crab-hippo monster of Zambia. Born from sorcery and magic, it swallows pebbles to become invisible. This uncanny creature is part of African folklore and adding hippos to any monster is understandable as they are one of the deadliest creatures on Earth! Hippos mouths open 150 degrees and they bite down with the weight of half a car. They attack boats and swimmers, killing an estimated 500 people a year! Crabs, well who would argue with those pincers carrying around not one, but two hippos! Nkala is a shadow-eating nightmare! Have you checked your shadow lately?

THUNDERBIRD

CANADA AND USA

Thunder cracks open the sky like thousands of drums beating. Lightning burns lines of white electric light across the grey clouds down onto the grassy plains, splitting trees apart and lighting up the whole scene bright as day. If science had not translated this spectacle as being caused by electricity, water molecules and air pressure, it would look like the work of something truly powerful.

Native Americans believe just that. Their storytelling and songs describe the mighty Thunderbird who controls a place called the Upper World. This magnificent creature is depicted in Native American art representing strength, protection and power. Up in the clouds, beyond the mountains, the Thunderbird surveys all the lands where its people live. Throwing lightning bolts from its eyes and making thunder from flapping its wings, it causes storms, bringing much-needed rain for crops or devastating floods. On its wings hang Thunderbirds' dogs! These are not normal dogs, but lightning bolt serpents with the heads of dogs that it shoots down to Earth to punish its enemies. And its three long tail feathers are supposed to represent time: the past, present and future of the world. It feeds on killer whales, which it scoops from the sea and fights in mid-air! Thunderbird can even remove its bird face like a mask and shrug off its beautiful feathers like a cape, to become human. As protective as it is, Native Americans never forget its awful vengeance. If it's displeased, Thunderbird will create avalanches, ice storms and even turn a whole village to stone.

It is no wonder that this magnificent creature sits on top of many totem poles with wings outstretched above the killer whale. But what could have inspired this mythical creature? The discovery of dinosaur bones in caves across the USA was made by Native America people. Prehistoric pterosaurs were gigantic flying reptiles with wingspans up to 10 metres wide, perhaps these flying beasts inspired the Thunderbird stories.

BANSHEE

OTHER NAMES Bean Nighe, Cyhyraeth

IRELAND

Ayeeeeeeeeeeeeeeeeeeeeeeeeeeeeeeeeeeeeeeeeeeeeeeeeeeeeeeeeeeee, ayeeeeeeeeeeeeeeeeeeeeeeeeeeeeee, sob, sob, ayeeeeeeeeeeeeeeeeeee eeeeee, gurgle, gasp, sniff.

Look out into the mist, can you see the grassy mound under the stricken tree? Who is that standing in a long grey dress and veil, so ghastly pale? She cries. Oh how she cries! Her red eyes are raw with crying. The shrill wail fills you with sadness. You try to shut out her sound, but it fills the air. Grief, death and bad luck travel on her voice. Glass shatters as her screams ring out.

If you hear her mournful wail in the dead of night, while travelling through the Irish countryside, then stop. You may want to block your ears, but it may be too late. That sound is a terrible warning, an omen of death that follows like a shadow. You have just encountered the Banshee. This mythological creature of despair dates back to the Norman era and is documented in many local legends, such as the Bunratty Banshee and the Banshee of Shane's Castle from the seventeenth century.

The Banshee is not a predatory monster, but her power is in her emotions. Her screams are the threat of death. Years ago, the job of grieving when someone died would be taken on by a group of women at funerals. The louder and more visible the sadness, the more important and missed the person was thought to be. In the eighth century, and throughout the following centuries, people faced losing loved ones through disease and war with a far greater regularity than now. The wailing Banshee was a fearful reminder that death was close. The superstitious, who thought they heard her voice on the wind, would hold their breath and hope illness or famine was not passing through their village. Banshees tell us a story about grief and fear. We do not want to hear her, yet she is there.

TROLL

OTHER NAMES Trullan, Trylla

ICELAND, NORWAY AND SWEDEN

Under every wooden bridge lives a troll. In every tall forest hides a troll. On every wind-blasted rocky landscape once lived a troll, or an army of trolls, who fought so long and hard that the sun eventually rose and turned them all to stone! There are trolls for every environment, in every Scandinavian country and within most fantasy books and films. Children have feared for the lives of the *Three Billy Goats Gruff* as they trip trap across the bridge to reach the lush meadow beyond, right over the troll who lurks underneath. Trolls are bad news.

These ancient creatures were first shared in spoken stories centuries ago. Norwegian Norse sagas spread these tales across the world. Trolls can be small or mountain-sized, hairy or bald, and knobbly or smooth. They love to fight and eat people. Trolls are shy of being seen and loathe certain noises. The worst sound to their huge ears are church bells clanging. Lightning and bright flashes of light terrify them, perhaps because sunlight is their enemy. If a troll is caught in daylight, its warty grey flesh will stiffen, crack and become stone, eventually weathering down to look like boulders and mounds. Trolltindene or Troll Peak, in central Norway, is famous for being the last resting place of a troll army. You can almost see the trolls' pained faces in the rock surfaces, softened by moss and lichens.

There have been many sightings of trolls, so many that it would take a whole book to note them all. People have glimpsed them in woodlands and mountains, they have attacked their cars and slimed their campsites.

Trolls bear a striking resemblance to Neanderthals, an early relative of humans, and some research imagines that modern humans' descriptions of the Neanderthals led to Troll folklore. Do you believe in Trolls? Not the flowing-haired disco-dancing singing ones, but the people-eating bridge lurkers?

UNDERWATER PANTHER

OTHER NAMES Great Lynx, Mishipeshu

CANADA AND USA

A skin hangs inside the tent of the Algonquian tribespeople. As the light from the entrance catches it, like a searchlight, you notice the incredible details of this uncanny creature. 'Is that a cat skin?' The tribe spokesperson shakes their head. 'Maybe a bull? It has horns!' 'No.' 'A serpent?' You can see scales, sharp dagger-like spikes along its back and a snake-like tail, but the main features look like a panther. 'What is it?' The tribesperson answers, 'Mishipeshu, the powerful underwater panther.'

This majestic creature is a large water being that appears in Native American paintings, looking like a spiky wildcat. These creatures exist in the stories and beliefs of the tribes that span the north-eastern woodlands and Great Lakes of North America. Tales even talk of them being caught by tribespeople, who hang the incredible skins in their tents.

Swimming in the deep waters of the Great Lakes, the Underwater Panther protected a valuable natural resource, the metal copper. The Native Americans were respectful of this precious material but some took more than their share. Tales tell of awful roars crossing the lake as copper-filled canoes rowed back to shore. The lake boiled from the Panther's vengeful anger, causing the boats to sink and returning the copper to the lakebed where it came from.

Great Underwater Wildcat, Underwater Panther, Great Lynx and the Fabulous Night Panther all conjure up images of a fantastical, mysterious animal. Its roars and hisses can cause terrible storms, ripping across the Great Lakes and creating dangerous whirlpools. Sightings of this beast describe seeing the large cat leaping and pouncing in the powerful swirls, as if running on a never-ending spiral staircase to the watery bottom of the lake.

According to folklore, its enemy is the Thunderbird, who rules the skies with power and majesty. These two creatures are the opposites of each other, but they are both very important beings from the indigenous Underworld. Their battle creates a balance, their conflict creates energy.

TE WHEKE A MUTURANGI

NEW ZEALAND

Do you have a pet? People choose all sorts of different animal companions; cats, dogs, rats, stick insects, hamsters, snakes, tortoises, rabbits ... what about an octopus? An octopus the size of a jumbo jet? That was the pet of choice for Muturangi, in the Māori myth of Kupe and Te Wheke!

Kupe was a Māori warrior and navigator from Ra'iatea, an island in French Polynesia, in the South Pacific Ocean. Fishing in the waters around the island to feed his community, Kupe found his nets were full of slime. Where were all the fish? Hunger was setting in and Kupe asked his wife, Kuramarotini, what could be happening? She said one word; *'wheke'*, octopus. Kupe shuddered, it must be huge to eat all the fish and produce gallons of slime! He knew who kept a giant octopus as a pet, his neighbour, Muturangi. Kupe went and asked Muturangi to control his pet. He selfishly replied, 'Let Te Wheke eat! He deserves the fish!' Kupe knew he must destroy the monster or starve. Gathering his family and Māori warriors, they sailed by *'waka'* – canoe – and lured Muturangi's pet across the sea, where it followed them like a fast, undulating island. Kupe rowed into deep water and fought this mighty beast. The fight was tremendous. Imagine the small canoes surrounded by whipping and flailing coils of tentacles, which tried to squeeze and smash them out of the water. Kupe eventually cut off the octopus's tentacles and killed the mighty Te Wheke a Muturangi! This battle would have been epic enough, but Kupe then spotted an undiscovered land. He named it Aotearoa – New Zealand!

Te Wheke a Muturangi is not only seen as a sea monster, it is also used to represent the navigation channels across the Pacific Ocean. Its long tentacles point and stretch across into new lands, unchartered back in early Māori history. Old maps always depicted the seas full of tentacled beasts. Are these helpful route-finders or monstrous enemies? Maybe they are both!

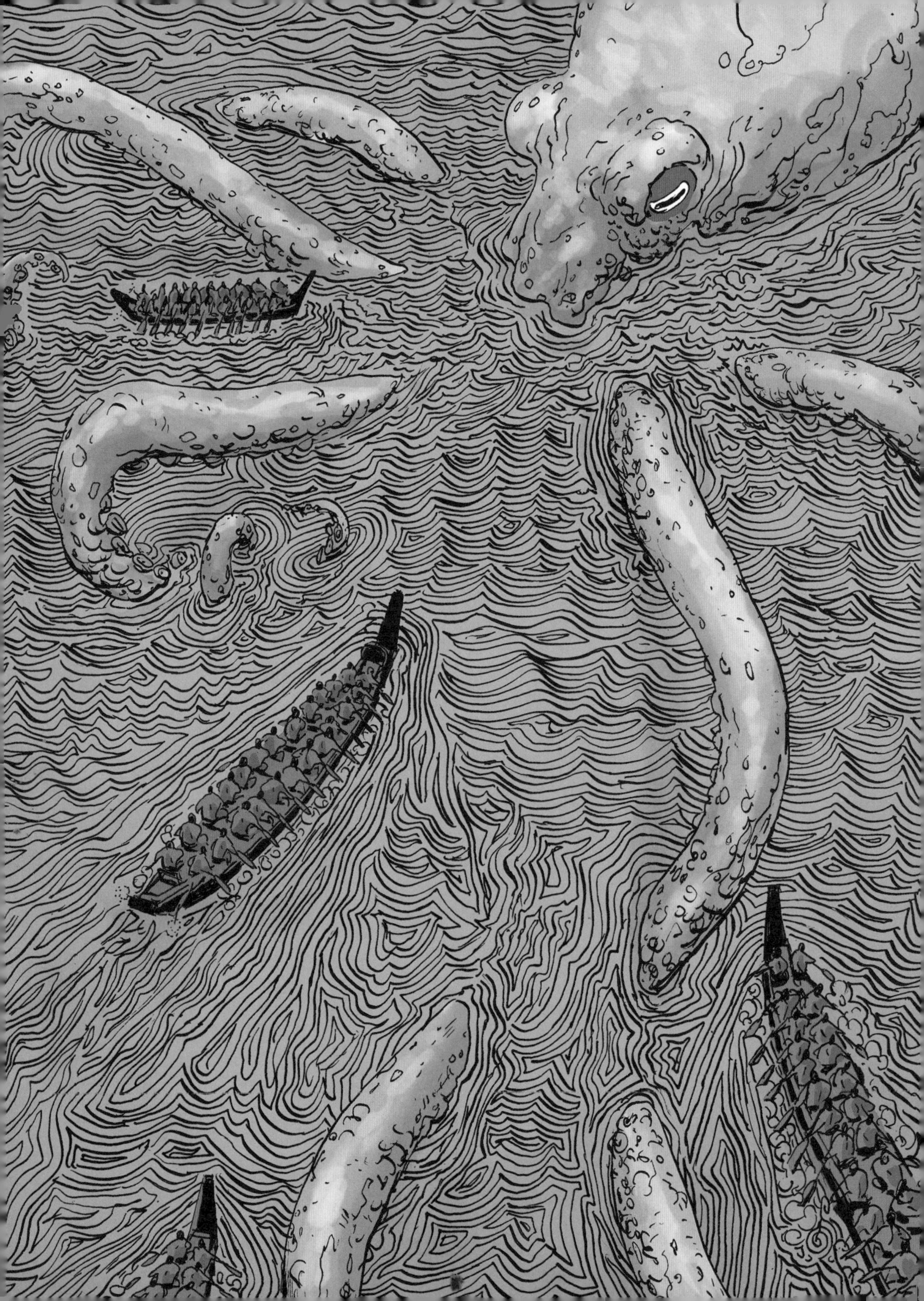

UCUMAR-ZUPAI

OTHER NAMES Ucu

ARGENTINA AND CHILE

The campfire's flames dance in the warm air, smoke curls up over the tents and disappears into the tall trees. As the logs hiss and blacken, you settle in to listen to the camper's story ...

'This place is special,' he holds up his arms to motion to the trees and sky, 'the Yungas forest is not only a wild, tropical, mountainous region, it is also home to something we cannot understand.' He sighs, poking the fire, making it leap. 'In these dense forests lives a wild man. To call him 'man' you may think it is human. But he, or she, stands taller than all of us, with glowing green eyes, matted thick fur and powerful limbs. It roams all over this region. Beware! For if you hear it scream you will never clear the sound from your ears. Its call roars through these forests, around the mountains, stunning wildlife and terrorising people.' He whispered, 'It is Ucumar-Zupai. And we will do well to keep watch for it while we make ourselves visible with the fire. It may want a midnight feast!'

You laugh and say goodnight, zipping up your tent, which is pitched in the forest clearing. You fall asleep lulled by the insect sounds ... a deafening roar cuts into your sleep:

UHU, UHU, UHU!

The trees around you shudder. You tear open your tent, and in the tree line you see it! A huge ape, eyes burning green and fangs. It opens its mouth and screams. Ucumar-Zupai looms over the camp and it is true, your ears will ring with 'Uhu' forever.

Ucumar-Zupai has been spotted and heard for many decades. A huge ape-like beast who screams in the forests and mountains of Argentina and Chile. Its half-a-metre-long footprint was found by a geologist 5,000 metres up in the Argentine Andes mountains. No known animals make that sound, what do you think it could be?

CANADA AND USA

Warning! This monster is deadly ... deadly cute! But it's also deadly mischievous, fast and magical.

Azeban, the trickster raccoon, belongs in the stories of the indigenous Abenaki and Penobscot tribes who live in New England, USA and southern Quebec, Canada. They use this very badly behaved monster to teach children lessons about how not to behave.

Your standard raccoon is already an incredibly cunning creature. They have been known to leave false trails up trees to dodge being captured and hold their paws up like a criminal when caught red handed! Raccoons are excellent at hiding and are as skilled in trees as they are on the ground. The tribespeople thought that raccoons were spirits of land, air and water. But Azeban is much more cunning than a typical raccoon. Myths describe him as a charming, naughty character that attempts to talk his way into getting food or outsmarting people. He can suddenly disappear and is as fast as lightning. In one tale, Azeban challenges a roaring waterfall to a shouting match. 'Oh, you think you can talk over me!?' he scoffs and tries to shout over the roar, but just a squeak comes out. He shouts and shouts, but his voice is too small. Eventually he shouts until he goes giddy and falls off the cliff!

Stories of proud, scheming and greedy Azeban are similar to fables told to children, such as *The Three Little Pigs* or *The Gingerbread Man*. They show what happens if you avoid hard work or open the door to the wolf! Things end badly.

Azeban is also like the Marvel Studios' character Rocket Raccoon. Both are clever, love to steal things and cause absolute mayhem. They are not cruel or uncaring though; they just have too much energy and love misbehaving.

This is a rare monster within this book; cute, not murderous and doesn't eat people, drink blood or hide in your cupboard. But if your fish goes missing at dinner and your bedroom has been ransacked, don't blame your siblings, it was probably Azeban!

YETI

OTHER NAMES Abominable Snowman, Meh-Teh

CHINA AND NEPAL

Do you believe in mysteries? Perhaps the most famous, searched for and documented monster mystery of all is the Yeti, or Abominable Snowman. This wild man of the snow has captivated explorers, scientists and children since the eighteenth century. Why? Dress warmly, you are travelling to the Himalayas to search for yourself ...

The highest mountain on Earth is above you. Everest, in the Himalayan mountains on the border of China and Nepal, stands at 8,850 metres shrouded by clouds. The air glitters with ice crystals as you begin your trek. It's well below freezing so every part of you is wrapped up. You are taking an old explorers route and, as you look over the Lhakpa La or Windy Gap, you still have much further to go. There! A huge footprint, as long as your arm, is pressed deep in the snow in front of you! The first Yeti footprint was reported on an 1887 expedition. You push ahead through snowstorms, pitching your tent on thick ice. It seems incredible that so many people embrace this peril to chase a monster.

Up, up, up you climb until the clouds are below you. You set camp 6,500 metres up in the sky, as high as planes fly! The night is terrible. You are freezing, and outside the tent screams and howls fill the darkness. You dare to peek out and there he is! Huge, white, hairy and prowling around the camp. You look upon the Abominable Snowman! How can he survive up here? He must be so lonely.

In the morning, you see huge footprints in the snow. You are now one of the many explorers to have captured a glimpse of the Yeti. You tell your Sherpa guide. He says, *'metoh-kangmi,'* meaning 'man-bear snow-man', then *'Yeti'*, meaning 'wild man'.

In 1951 Eric Shipton photographed the famous Yeti footprint, which sparked worldwide interest. In 1960, Everest explorer Sir Edmund Hillary spent nine months searching for the creature! But still the Yeti remains the most secretive and mysterious monster of them all!

LA CIGUAPA

DOMINICAN REPUBLIC

Do you love to hear bird song? Sweet twilling, chirping and twittering filling the air at dawn, and softening to silence at dusk. Have you ever woken at night, in complete darkness and heard a bird singing? It is a strange and haunting sound, lonely and beautiful, separated from all the other background noises.

If you were up in the Caribbean mountain forests of the Dominican Republic in the dead of night, you may hear a chirping, whining call from the tree tops. If you listen to this beautiful sound DO NOT look up to find the bird. You may find something very strange indeed.

La Ciguapa, a mountain siren, is above you, kicking her legs through her long, silken hair. With deep-blue skin like the night sky, her large, glassy eyes stare down, cascades of long hair cover her whole body like a sheet and her feet ... well, her feet are on backwards.

This nocturnal creature is rarely seen. She appears different to different people and is almost impossible to catch. To follow her footprints in the dirt, you would be going in the wrong direction as her feet leave a reverse imprint. To capture La Ciguapa you must go out during a full moon accompanied by a white cinqueño dog. This dog has extra toes on its paws and will help to lure her, but you must not let her chirp and sing to you. Much like the half-bird, half-woman sirens of the sea, La Ciguapa's song is deadly. She looks so calm perched on the mountainside or reclining in the trees, but she will mesmerise you and eat you. You knew there must be something monstrous about her.

There have been several monsters throughout folklore with backwards-facing feet. They are seemingly created to trick onlookers and explain how people can get lost following tracks. Nobody is sure of the origin of La Ciguapa, but she is one of the Dominican Republic's most famous mythical creatures.

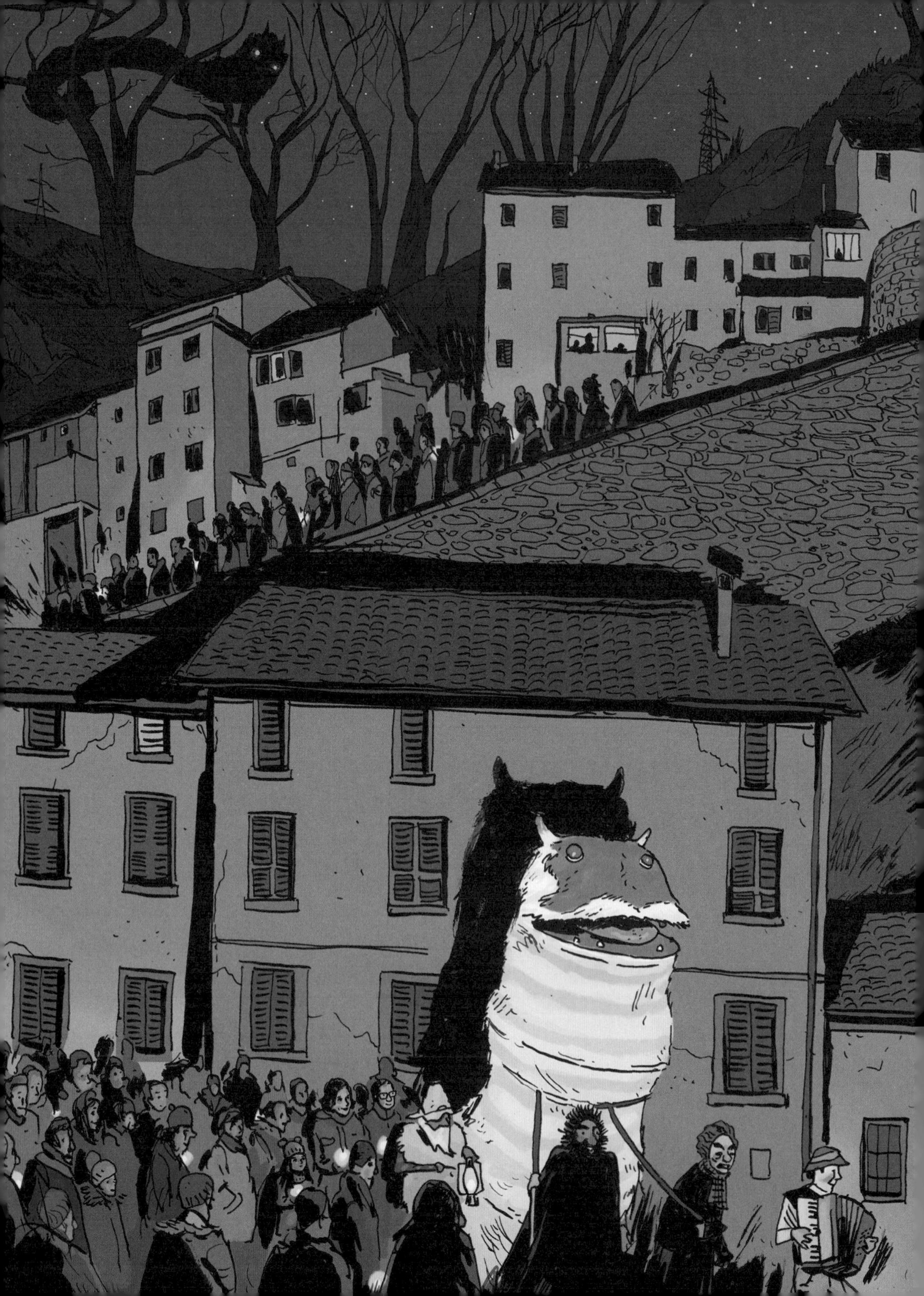

BADALISC

ITALY

The townspeople of Andrista, in Lombardy, Italy make their way through the steep, winding streets and out into the woods beyond. Torches blaze, voices are hushed and a drum beats rhythmically as they go on a monster hunt ...

Into the dark woods they stream, spreading out among the trees on the mountainside, all looking for the monster that has appeared every January for decades. The drums beat, excitement builds and a pair of glowing red eyes watch from the trees. Someone shouts, '*Là! Eccolo*! – There! There he is!' and the ritual of Festa del Badalisc begins! A colourful cast of characters wearing masks and costumes step forwards from the crowd. There's the young man – *il giovani*, the old man – *un signore anziano*, the old woman – *la signora anziana*, the young lady – *signora* and the hunchback – *un torro gobetto*, as well as witches and bearded shepherds. They begin the tradition of capturing the Badalisc!

Covered with goat skins, the Badalisc is tall with horns, a huge gaping mouth and his eyes flash on and off. On and off. Hang on! This is all fake! The Badalisc isn't a real monster, it's a man dressed up! The crowd cheer as he is caught and led to the town square. Here, the hunchback character and the monster pretend to fight. Next, a rhyming speech is read out that is written by the monster, but he doesn't speak. It's full of cruel jokes and gossip about the townspeople – the naughty, rude Badalisc! For two days the townspeople dance and feast with the monster as their guest of honour!

The Badalisc celebration is linked to religious traditions, but it also has roots in local folklore. Each year, it brings the community together and the performance reminds them to be kind and forgiving.

After the merriment, costumes are hung up and the Badalisc is set free, until next winter. As the town sleeps, up in the forest, looking over the Alpine town, red eyes glow in the trees. Not battery-powered. It slithers into the darkness.

MUMMY

EGYPT

You're sat in front of a mummy in a glass case, sketching the Egyptian pharaoh's death mask. The museum seems empty. You look at the bandaged body; there is a dead king in there! But it's a long way from Egypt now. A very old man is watching you draw. 'You like that mummy?' he asks. 'You wouldn't if it chased you.' The old man continues ...

I was studying archaeology in Tanis, Egypt. I still have sand in my jacket pockets from 1939. We discovered the sealed entrance to a tomb and blasted through it. The air was stale, trapped for thousands of years. In the lamp light, it was like illuminating a box of sweets. There were such treasures and further down, a box. A box that archaeologists dream about! The coffin, or sarcophagus, of your mummy there. Like pass the parcel, it was opened and layers of decorated lids were unpacked. I felt guilty. The dead would not want to be disturbed. Wary of grave robbers, I stayed alone overnight and watched over the tomb. There were hours of silence with just my lamp flickering ... then the mummy sat up. Please, believe me. It sat up and my heart stopped. I stumbled against the painted walls, wiping off centuries of hieroglyphs. The mummy stared ahead, and just as I reached the door, it moaned and stepped out of the coffin. I ran! It followed, gurgling and shuffling. The guards outside laughed at me. But the next day, they found the mummy with his arms outstretched. He almost got me.

You listen, appalled. The museum guard makes you both jump as he announces the museum is closing. You offer the drawing to the old man. 'No thank you,' he smiles, 'I see him in my nightmares.'

Thanks to the Curse of Tutankhamun, horror films and books, it's no surprise that mummies have become such a classic monster. A bandaged, preserved body within a pyramid, surrounded by gold and a curse to scare away intruders. Mummy's are the perfect historical horror story!

KRAMPUS

OTHER NAMES Black Peter, Horned God of the Witches, Knecht Ruprecht

NORTHERN EUROPE

Snowy rooftops. Fire embers glow in the hearth. The black sky seems even darker above the blanket of snow that covers everything. Just the twinkling fairy lights illuminate the houses on this winter's night. From the soft nest of bed, you listen. Your heart is beating loudly; is that the jingle of bells? A sleigh scraping on the snowy roof? It is too early for Father Christmas, unless he has confused the date?

Have you been good this year? You have! Well that could be the sound of Father Christmas coming early to leave gifts, fill stockings and spread joy.
You haven't? Then that must be the sound of someone entirely different paying you a visit ...

You realise it's not bells you can hear, but chains clinking. You peer through the curtain and see a silhouette on the white lawn. It's part-man, part-goat and part-nightmare! Running back to bed, you begin to shiver. You pull the covers over your head and hold your breath. That isn't Father Christmas. He doesn't come early, and it's only December 5th. Ho Ho No! It's Krampus! This Christmas monster only visits naughty children. He snorts and stamps his cloven feet. On his furry back is a large basket, just big enough to pop children in. His long, pointed tongue protrudes from between fangs! Tonight is *Krampusnacht*, or Krampus Night, and he's here to deliver birch twigs to children as a warning to behave.

Across northern Europe, Krampus is as much a celebrated and loved part of Christmas tradition as Father Christmas himself. He is the dark to Father Christmas's light; he will punish where Father Christmas rewards. In Germany, Croatia and Slovenia, people host *Krampuslauf*, a popular event where hundreds of Krampuses run through the streets scaring the crowds, wearing carved wooden masks, huge fur coats and pretending to whip the screaming delighted onlookers.

You better watch out, you better be good or Krampus will visit in his fur and fanged hood!

GLOSSARY

ABORIGINAL A person or people who were the first to live in a country before other settlers moved in, such as the Australian Aboriginal peoples.

APEX PREDATOR An animal at the top of the food chain. Apex predators are not hunted by other animals and include lions and polar bears.

BASQUE The people who live in the western Pyrenees mountains, which run along the French-Spanish border.

CANNIBALISM When an animal eats another animal of its own kind.

CRETACEOUS A time period from approximately 145–66 million years ago, when dinosaurs such as the tyrannosaurus rex existed.

GENETICIST A scientist or expert who studies genes, the parts of cells that control physical appearance and behaviour.

GORGON A female snake-haired creature from ancient Greece whose stare turned people to stone.

INDIGENOUS People or animals that live in the place they originated from, rather than arriving from another place.

JINN A good or bad spirit in Arabian and Muslim mythology, who can appear as human or animal.

MEGALITH A large stone that makes up part of a prehistoric monument, such as Stonehenge. Megaliths are found across the world.

MESOPOTAMIA An old historical area of south-western Asia.

MUTATE When a living thing changes or develops new characteristics, often physical, from the ones they originally had.

ORGANISM A single living thing such as a plant, animal or cell.

PAREIDOLIA When people see faces and pictures in things that aren't really there, such as faces in clouds.

PERSIA An old name for Iran, which is in the Middle East.

PLATEAU An area of flat, high ground.

PRISM A see-through object, such as glass or water droplets, which separates white light that passes through it into a rainbow of colours.

SPORE A tiny one-celled living thing that can make more of itself, produced by bacteria, fungi and various plants.

TAOIST A person believing in the ancient Chinese religion Taoism, which believes people should lead a simple life.

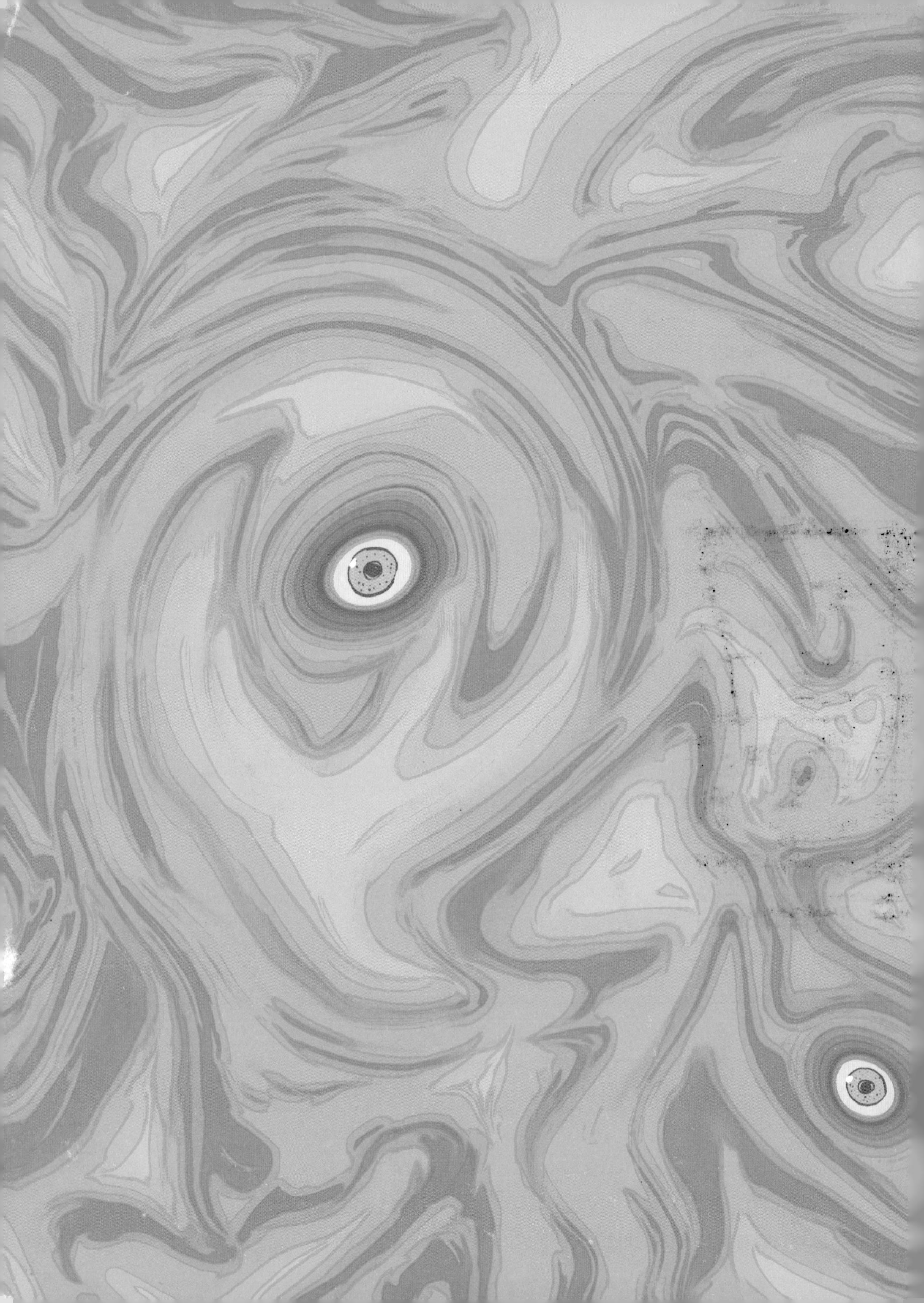